W9-ADS-280

CARMELITE MONASTERY
LIBRARY
SARANAC LAKE, N Y

# ESTHER BLONDIN
## PROPHET FOR TODAY

Christine Mailloux, S.S.A.

Éditions Paulines
Les Sœurs de Sainte-Anne

B
Blondin

illa E Originally published as

*Esther Blondin, prophète pour aujourd'hui*

Éditions Paulines, Montreal, 1987.

Translated into English by Sister Eileen Gallagher, S.S.A.

Phototypesetting: *Les Éditions Paulines*

Cover: *Tony Graf*

ISBN 2-89039-646-0

Legal deposit — 4th quarter 1989
Bibliothèque nationale du Québec
National Library of Canada

© 1989 Les Éditions Paulines
      3965, boul. Henri-Bourassa Est
      Montréal, QC, H1H 1L1

      Les Sœurs de Sainte-Anne
      1950, rue Provost
      Lachine, QC, H8S 1P7

All rights reserved for all countries.

*To the memory of*
*Sister Marie Jean de Pathmos, S.S.A.,*
*whose writings opened for me*
*the door of yesterday's history*
*that is so close*
*to our present struggle*
*for truth and justice*
*in a nonviolent way.*

# Acknowledgements

*To Sister Eileen Gallagher, S.S.A., who willingly, lovingly and reverently translated the French version of this book.*

*To all who encouraged me by their trust, criticisms and professional guidance, my sincere gratitude.*

C.M.

# CONTENTS

# Foreword

*Utopia shared is the springboard of history.*

Hélder Câmara

This work might have been entitled «*Prophets of Yesterday and Today*» or «*Family Portraits*» since it treats of the prophesying of Esther Blondin alongside that of Gandhi, Oscar Romero, Martin Luther King, and Hélder Câmara. But, the specific purpose of this book is to put into relief the figure of Esther Blondin. And at the same time, it proposes to show the appropriateness of the message her whole life gave us. The title chosen underscores this twofold purpose.

It must be said, at the outset, that this is an audacious point of view. What, indeed, is there in common between this 19th Century Quebec woman and Gandhi, or Martin Luther King? At first glance, in fact, nothing seems to bring them even close. They were of different eras; they had no cultural contact, social or political; they did not share official membership in any one Church, religion, language, or race; they did not even accomplish the same work. In fact, they were so different, that they could be contrasted. Esther Blondin overcame her illiteracy at age twenty; whereas, at that age, the other prophets were pursuing university studies. She spent the greater part of her life in the most complete anonymity, while they were famous in their lifetime.

Nevertheless, whatever distance separates these men and this woman, there can be no denying their profound resemblance. The prophetic dynamism with which they carried out their respective missions in different eras and milieux unequivocally characterizes all of them. They belong in fact to a spiritual family which the present work seeks not so much to define as to draw out in vigorous lines. So came the idea of writing a basic biography of Esther Blondin using as support biographies the lives of Gandhi, Romero, Câmara and King. The reading alone of these lives animated as they are by a common powerful inspiration brings

13

out certain fundamental traits: a commitment to justice, authenticity in their speech, a tragic destiny, nonviolence that forgives and an openness to the future.[1]

This book is not the result of an exhaustive study of prophecy in order to define it. It is rather the fruit of personal reflection on the real life experience of specific prophets. This fact reveals one of its strong points and one of its limitations. As a definition it could have been successfully completed by other more theological works. Nevertheless some key elements of Biblical prophecy will be found in this book. They are drawn from Xavier Léon Dufour's *Dictionnaire du Nouveau Testament*.[2]

It can be noted, as well, that Esther Blondin is the only woman in this book, even though there is no lack of women prophets today. But, women prophets are not the focus of this book. Such a limitation is no more significant than that among the five, there are four whites to one black; and four Christians to one Hindu.

It must be emphasized, however, that a study of women prophets, including Esther Blondin, would arouse great interest. The reason for this is that women constantly face social constraints, and cultures cast them into traditional roles. Their prophesying is no exception to these pressures, whether it be the forms their prophecy takes or its contents. From this perspective, Esther Blondin's story would be up-to-date and particularly significant.

Her lifestyle, as a woman, might seem outmoded in some respects. On the other hand, it can provide food for valuable thought, and more so because it is from the past. And so, the one whom tradition designates as "martyr of silence"[3] appears

---

[1] The appendix lists biographical sketches on each of the persons in this work. It is suggested that readers start the book with these, and return to them as the need arises. (C.M.)

[2] See Xavier Léon Dufour, *"Dictionnaire du Nouveau Testament"*, 2e édition, pp. 448-449. The author says that God puts His plan of salvation into action through the Biblical prophet. He speaks through prophets, calling for a change of actual situations. Through prophets, He sometimes foretells events. The author, also, makes it a point to stress that a tragic destiny is typical for prophets.

[3] On this subject, see the biography written in 1956 by Father Eugène

14

today more like a woman standing up in the Church and in the society of her own day. The silence to which she was confined was the consequence of her mission as foundress, a mission whose character was essentially prophetic. For her tragic destiny was rooted in Esther's very mission. And she lived it in the "Church," that is, "in her own country" as it is said in the Gospel.[4]

The scandal aspect of her story can be shocking. The same can be said of all the prophets: Gandhi and Martin Luther King were assassinated by one of their own people. Oscar Romero, also, would be disparaged by his own colleagues. Hélder Câmara would be ostracized within the Church. All of them shared the lot of Jesus of Nazareth, even the shame of His Cross. The foundress of the Sisters of Saint Anne did not escape that spiritual reality emerging on Easter morning.

The present work deals with a reality that is deeply rooted in the history of Québec, which at the beginning of the 19th Century was still called "Lower Canada."[5] The French Canadians living there were still suffering the consequences of the conquest of 1760, but they resisted the policies of assimilation, social, linguistic, and religious, that the British tried to impose on them.[6] This population, which was very largely rural, lived in an uncertain situation and was marked by real intellectual indigence, which had been growing worse under English domination: illiteracy,

---

Nadeau, O.M.I., under the title *Martyre du Silence*. The English translation by Sister Mary Camilla, S.S.A., is under the title *The life of Mother Mary Ann Foundress of the Sisters of Saint Ann (1809-1890)*.

[4] See Matthew 13:57, Luke 4:24, and John 4:44.

[5] Lower Canada would not become the Province of Quebec until the beginning of Confederation, July 1, 1867.

[6] On the policial, ecclesiastic, and scholastic situation in 19th Century Quebec, see Sister Marie Jean de Pathmos, S.S.A., *"Canonisation de la servante de Dieu Marie-Esther Sureau dit Blondin, Dossier sur la vie et les vertus,* pp. 1-27. From now on, reference to this work will be the following part of the title: *Dossier sur la vie et les vertus.* The quotations from this community work will be freely translated into English because both the author and the translator belong to the Community of the Sisters of Saint Anne. For the same reasons, we will adopt this procedure with regards to another work, the *Positio super introductione causæ.*

15

scarcity of teachers, shortage of books, rupture of cultural links with France. The Royal Institute of 1801 for the establishment of free schools and the advancement of science proved to be a trap for French Canadians. The purpose of this Institute was to anglicize and protestantize them. That was why they refused to send their children to school. It would be only in 1824 that the Law of Fabrique Schools would be passed, authorizing parishes to establish and maintain primary schools at their own expense. This system, which paralleled the Royal Institute, proved to be burdensome. It was only in 1829 that an important step was taken to establish a more adequate school system. The Assembly Schools Law then inaugurated public instruction and permitted the opening of 1500 schools in less than seven years.[7] After further hazards, during the time of great political tension[8], they finally succeeded in passing the Confessional Schools Law in 1846, which established the school system that lasted until 1960. But legislation in aid of French Canadians does not imply the elimination of illiteracy and poverty. In fact, they prevailed in the countryside of Lower Canada in the mid-19th Century. Yet, the Vaudreuil region, where Esther Blondin went in 1833, was not the most disadvantaged. It had maintained a local, independent, scholastic organization, which had escaped the political storm of 1837. This was due to the efforts of one of its pastors, Father Paul Loup Archambault.[9]

The Church of Lower Canada at the beginning of the 19th Century, seems, at first, to have been marked by a strong conservative mentality. This could have been partly due to an attitude

---

[7] *Ibid.,* p. 20.

[8] A reference to the nationalist insurrection of 1837-38 when the Patriots were defeated.

[9] Father Paul Loup Archambault was pastor of Vaudreuil for forty-two years, that is, from 1816-1858. He set aside a good part of his revenue for the education of children. He saw to the construction of schools in his parish and hired teachers, men and women, paying them from his own funds. Esther Blondin joined Suzanne Pineault to teach in one of these schools, as a lay teacher, from 1833 to 1850. It was there that she founded her community in 1850.

of introspection in the face of British attempts to assimilate the French. The insufficient formation of the clergy reinforced this mentality. Theirs was a narrow-minded education in a closed environment. This clergy was, nevertheless, part of the most educated minority in the population, which accounted for the influence they enjoyed. In general, also, they gave evidence of a remarkable moral life. For an example of the religious mentality which marked 19th Century Québec, we need only review the contents of the first Provincial Council held in 1851. This Council dealt with liturgy, education, and discipline, among other things. For the liturgy, the ritual, the missal and Gregorian chant were standardized to Roman criteria. In education, the Council made a radical separation between the Church and adherers of other religions. It voices mistrust of the ability of lay people to ensure the religious and moral instruction of youth. And it insisted on the separation of sexes in schools. As for discipline, it regulated dances, entertainment, intermingling among the young, and it prohibited secret societies. Furthermore, the population of Québec was typically rural. This factor favoured the development of traditions that were passed down from one generation to the next. All these facts give a better understanding of the stability and religious conservatism, which marked the era in which Esther Blondin was born.[10]

It was through her family that Esther, as a child, received the heritage of her Christian faith, as it was lived in her milieu. She was the third of twelve children, seven of whom died in infancy, and was very young when she learned from her parents how to pray.[11] Her father, Jean Baptiste Blondin (1781-1853), and her mother, Marie Rose Limoges (1780-1862), were farmers in the area around Terrebonne, a village situated about 30 kilometers from Montreal. Unless we consider the poverty and the illiteracy of her family, there is nothing particular to note in Esther

---

[10] These reflections on the Canadian Church of the 19th Century were inspired by a course in history given at the Faculty of Theology of the University of Montreal by Professor Lucien Lemieux, in 1978.

[11] On the subject of Esther Blondin's childhood and youth, see Sister Marie Jean de Pathmos, S.S.A., *Dossier sur la vie et les vertus,* pp. 28-42.

Blondin's childhood. Still, these did leave their mark on her, possibly making her more sensitive to these privations in others. Historical documents point out Esther's delicate health and a moral and psychological crisis that she went through during her adolescence. Psychiatrists Henri Samson, S.J., and Joseph Géraud, P.S.S., who studied this crisis, are of the opinion that it was due to a lack of sexual education and to a kind of moral rigorism often found at that time.[12] They emphasized also that she proved herself psychologically very normal, indeed particularly strong, to have lived in astounding serenity the very turbulent events of her long life. At age 19, no doubt with the intention of helping her family, the young woman went into domestic service with a Terrebonne merchant. A year later, her services were hired by the Sisters of Congregation of Notre Dame who ran a school in the village. From January 1830, one of the sisters began to teach her after work hours. Two years later she requested admission to the Congregation. This was the result of the progress that Esther had made in learning, the contact she had had with a religious community of educators, and the call, which she had discerned as from God. She stayed there several months, but because of her poor health, she was sent home to her family. The spiritual influences, then, that marked Esther Blondin came from her family, from the atmosphere of Church where she grew up, and from the religious community where she had spent some time. These influences were unvaried, and so she developed fundamental values. Some of these virtues that grew within her were piety and the seeking out and submission to the will of God. As well, she advanced in the way of respect and obedience to established authority, honesty and uprightness. Added to these were a strict moral code and asceticism. We shall see how the prophetic Spirit moved the future foundress beyond the rigidity and the limitations of these values, as they were transmitted and lived in 19th Century Québec.

---

[12] See *Ibid.*, pp. 32-33. It was in this capacity of expert at the Sacred Congregation for Causes of the Saints that Father Joseph Géraud gave his opinion on the psychological difficulties that Esther Blondin experienced.

Lastly, we can note the determining influence which Bishop Bourget had on Esther Blondin. He was to be her shepherd and her confidant during the crucial years of foundation.[13] This second bishop of Montreal was a man of deep faith and extraordinary piety. His pastoral letters are ample witness to his devotion to the Eucharist, to the Passion of Christ, and to the Virgin Mary. The bishop was also recognized for his austerity. His concept of suffering was sometimes tinged by Jansenism and by the romanticism of his era. As we note in the letters he sent to the communities, religious life, to him, was a life of immolation. The spirituality of Saint Ignatius, founder of the Jesuits, also left its special mark on him. We know that he followed the Spiritual Exercises at the time of his first trip to Rome in 1841. We know, too, that his life was enriched by it, and that he prepared rules for Esther Blondin's community that were of Ignatian inspiration. So it is not surprising that he gave such importance to the final end of all things; that is, the glory of God and the salvation of souls. The means he used or suggested to arrive at that end, his methods of prayer and discernment, examen of conscience, rules, all follow naturally from this concept of spirituality. As for his concept of authority, it was steeped in the sacred, and this explains his unreasonable demands for submission and obedience.

These are, briefly, the context and the influence that formed Esther Blondin. It is good to keep these elements in mind, in order to appreciate more accurately the innovative character of her work, and to understand more deeply the history of her mission. Thus, the distance imposed on us by time will not obscure her prophetic dynamism. This is what brings her close to Gandhi, Romero, King and Câmara, as though by design. For if their tasks were different, they were certainly walking in the same direction.

---

[13] On the spiritual side of Bishop Bourget see *The First Rules of the Sisters of Saint Anne* as set forth and annotated by Louise Roy, S.S.A., pp. 11-17, and Léon Pouliot, S.J., *Monseigneur Bourget et son temps,* III, pp. 179-180.

# Chapter 1

# A Prophetic Way of Acting

*God is continually asking me to found a community which will devote itself to the interests and the education of the rural poor.*

Esther Blondin

*How often are our lives characterized by a high blood pressure of creeds and an anemia of deeds.*

Martin Luther King

The most striking aspect of a mission of prophetic character is the energy displayed in a concrete action. It seems that many prophets are men and women of action. Deeply rooted in their culture and their times, they confront injustices, those hidden mines, wherever they go. But it is their intervention that is explosive; and so, they are soon labelled as disturbers of the peace, that is, a threat to the status quo. Yet, because they are passionately committed to justice, they do not give up, even though carrying out their purpose is never easy.

## The Origin of a Mission

Such was Esther Blondin. She was born into the rural life of 19th Century Québec society and had experiences which prepared her for her mission. There was her own illiteracy at age 20. There was her brief association as a novice with the Sisters of the Congregation of Notre Dame. Then, there was her employment in Vaudreuil as a village teacher. In these ways she widened her horizons, and certain other realities began to take on more weight in her estimation of values. Esther was not yet thirty when she was exercising a remarkable influence in the Vaudreuil school, which she ran with her friend Suzanne Pineault. Later circumstances placed her at the head of the school; and as the number of children increased, she hired two assistants whom she trained herself.[1] In fifteen years, then, this young woman progressed from her position of daughter in a large, illiterate family to that of school directress, following a futile effort to join a

---

[1] See *Positio super introductione Causæ,* pp. 325 and 327. This reference will henceforth be called simply *Positio.*

religious community of educators. The road she walked was taking a definite direction.

At the end of the school year 1846-1847, history records that she fell ill and was obliged to take some time off to rest. For months, Esther reflected on her experience, questioned herself on her life and her activity, and prayed long. That which was emerging from her, very mysteriously, ripened in solitude. The faces of those she was educating peopled this time of forced inaction. Her powerlessness, at that time, might have made her more open to the distress of certain other children. Those who were too poor to go to school, or too far from it, could have stirred her pity at that time. Her thoughts might have turned towards those who could not receive sufficient formation for lack of competent teachers. Was her heart stirred by the plight of those who were deprived of the necessary catechism to prepare them for the sacraments?[2] She would be concerned that they would not grow up to live their Christian faith appropriately. One thing is certain. Esther at that moment was fighting a painful battle, similar to that of many of the prophets. On the one hand, she feared not grasping what it was God wanted of her. On the other hand, she glimpsed the sufferings she would have to endure along the unknown path where she felt called to travel. "Finally", said Father Aristide Brien who recorded her testimony, "she believed she understood, beyond a doubt, the Divine voice making itself heard within her heart."[3] At thirty-eight, she confided to Father Paul Loup Archambault, pastor of Vaudreuil: "I have no resources. God wants to do everything. He keeps asking me to found a community devoted to the interests and the instruction of the poor of the countryside. There is a void to be filled there. I understand that Divine Providence is committed to reveal the means that He alone knows, and that He will manifest in His own time."[4] When she communicated this project to her brother Jean Baptiste, he tried to dissuade her. But Esther remained firm "because", she said, "God wants it."

[2] See *Ibid.,* p. 331.

[3] *Ibid.,* p. 328.

[4] *Ibid.,* pp. 328-329.

# The Prophetic Choice

Her task, then, was to found a religious community of educators, who would further the rights of poor children to instruction and to a Christian education. With these pressing needs in her environment, Esther felt called to commit herself. At that time, in 19th Century Québec, this was particularly significant. She felt that God Himself was urging her to act and, finally, she could resist Him no longer. She mustered her courage and went to seek approval for her project from Bishop Ignace Bourget, then Bishop of the Diocese of Montreal. This step and many others[5] that challenged this very modest woman led her to a September morning in 1850. With four companions that she had recruited, she "promised freely and willingly to the Divine Majesty, the vows of poverty, chastity, obedience, and the instruction of children for the rest of her life."[6] Her love of God brought her to serve the rights of her most deprived brothers and sisters.

Esther, who had become Mother Marie Anne, undertook her foundation boldly. She wished to teach and to educate boys as well as girls, including other students. She intended to reach the most deprived, those who needed remedial help, the illiterate who were approaching adulthood. Pastors as well as parishioners took a negative view of this desire. Indeed, the mentality of the day was that men should teach adolescent boys and that women should take care of young girls, in separate schools. Father Archambault, moreover, had warned Esther as early as 1848: "We do not wish to conceal from you that the undertaking seemed rash, at first, subversive, and contrary to the principles

---

[5] One other step that Esther took was her discreet recruiting in the summer of 1848. She assembled six young girls from, or around, Vaudreuil. On the evening of September 6, 1848, they began together a retreat to inaugurate their project. Four of them would be in the first group to make profession: Julienne Ladouceur, Justine Poirier, Salomé Véronneau, and Suzanne Pineault. It was she who had invited Esther to come and work with her at the school in Vaudreuil in 1833.

[6] *Positio,* p. 750.

of sound morality. The Church has always opposed these types of schools, and if today she is open to them, it is through harsh necessity, because she sees in them less evil than to leave the young any longer in lay hands."[7] Even though Bishop Bourget consented to this daring project, Esther perceived his objections. She wrote to him in 1851: "Before speaking to you about it, I recommended the whole affair to God. I have the greatest hope that Your Grace will not oppose it. I have heard from a reliable source that my community will not be permitted to teach children of both sexes beyond the age of ten. If this is so, I consider the goal I aimed for to have been missed. It is the poor who appealed to my zeal and my charity (...) It is certain that the commissioners will not want to employ sisters if the children cannot attend school up to the age required by law. Please forgive me, Your Grace, for the tone of pain and grief in this letter."[8] There was nothing aggressive about Esther Blondin's boldness. Rather, it was a kind of freedom and non-conformism where the rights and the good of children and youth were at stake.[9].

Some elements of Esther's experience stood out already. In the light of her personal situation of ignorance, of her schooling

---

[7] *The Correspondence of Mother Marie Anne,* Letter from the Pastor Paul Loup Archambault to Marie Esther Sureau dit Blondin and her companions, September 13, 1848, p. 16. On the prejudice of the time, we must also mention a circular letter that Bishop Bourget addressed to his priests on September 3, 1852. "We will not allow men to run schools for girls. They are in themselves dangerous and immoral. The commissioners, teachers, fathers and mothers who refuse to conform to this rule should not be absolved," quoted in *The First Rules of the Sisters of Saint Anne* written and annotated by Louise Roy, S.S.A., and translated by Florence Chevalier, S.S.A., and Margaret Flanagan, S.S.A., page 99, note 6.

[8] *The Correspondence of Mother Marie Anne,* Letter to Bishop Bourget, July 15, 1851, p. 30.

[9] In fact, the foundress would not see her dream of mixed schools realized until the sisters were established in the West and in the United States. Her project could not take shape in Québec because, as early as 1854, the Provincial Council of Québec withdrew all possibility of action in this area. On this subject, see Sister Marie Jean de Pathmos, S.S.A., — *Dossier sur la vie et les vertus,* pp. 94 and 161, and Léon Pouliot, *S.J., Monseigneur Bourget et son temps,* III, p. 76, note 2.

in abeyance for so long, and of her contact with so many children and youth deprived of education, she felt more and more clearly and irresistibly the call to commit herself effectively to their service. She was caught up in the mystery of this call. God Himself, she was convinced, was pleading with her to act in a concrete way, regardless of the conformism which tolerated such an unjust state of affairs.

## The Firmly Rooted Commitment of the Prophets

It seems that prophetic missions arise from an actual situation, from the foaming and seething of life itself. Closer to our own time, *Mahatma* Gandhi, himself awakened by the painful experience he had lived in South Africa, was burning with zeal to achieve for his compatriots a "humanitarian and national service"[10] capable of freeing them not only from the yoke of English colonialism, but especially from the internal divisions which were undermining their strength and their dignity. And yet, he affirmed, "I have no special revelation of God's will (...), God never appears to you in person but in action."[11] Such an imperative, coming from a real situation, challenges the prophet to commitment and opens up to him an experience of God in direct line with the one offered by the Gospel.

Oscar Romero, too, sensed a similar call in a totally different context. He perceived through the tragic events that he witnessed the urgency of acting as a shepherd. Following the assassination of the Jesuit Rutilio Grande, on May 12, 1977, there was increased violence against peasants and committed Christians. It was then that the new archbishop of San Salvador entered wholeheartedly, with utmost courage, into a very compromising service of his brothers and sisters whose human dignity was being condemned. He explained: "The Latin-American bishops at Medellin directed

---

[10] Louis Fisher, *The Life of Mahatma Gandhi,* p. 151.

[11] *Ibid.,* p. 303.

the evangelization of our continent toward the service of human rights and the betterment of human beings. They felt it to be an authentic summons of the Spirit, one from which the Church could not turn away: 'a muted cry pours from the throats of millions... asking their pastors for a liberation that reaches them from nowhere else'." [12]

On the same continent, Hélder Câmara was one day pushed against the wall in a brotherly way by a French bishop participating in the Eucharistic Congress in Rio de Janeiro. From this meeting with Bishop Pierre Gerlier, he opened his eyes to the misery of the *favelas* in the big cities of Brazil and he decided to do something about it: "Let us press on without delay with the task of development as a Christian means of evangelization. What value can there be in venerating pretty images of Christ, or even recognizing His disfigured face in that of the poor, if we fail to identify Him with the human being who needs to be rescued from his underdeveloped condition." [13]

On his part, Martin Luther King, the Baptist Minister, discovered his prophetic vocation in the very situation he shared with his own people, racism; in it he risked his own comfortable circumstances, his security and his family. "My creed is service of God and therefore of humanity," [14] he could have said with Gandhi.

Always the same emphasis, the same realism, the same faith in God Who urges the prophets to effective action, so that the rights of the most deprived and the most exploited be reestablished. This seems to be how their missions are born.

---

[12] Oscar Romero, *Voice of the Voiceless,* pp. 163-164.

[13] Hélder Câmara, *The Church and Colonialism. The Betrayal of the Third World,* pp. 11-12.

[14] Mahatma Gandhi, *The Collected Works of Mahatma Gandhi,* XXV, p. 260.

# The Developing Action

From the time of her founding the community, Esther Blondin blazed trails in beginnings. First of all, she governed her little community for four years. These years of planting and growing proved to be rich with a dynamism that was given a special direction by the service she would be sharing with a growing number of followers. One of her contemporaries wrote that during this time, the foundress sometimes asked her sisters to "pray (...) that the community will grow according to God's plan."[15] In this perspective, she discerned vocations to her community, formed novices carefully, and sought the spiritual help of a priest. She wrote to Bishop Bourget: "I kept putting off (writing to you) but today, I feel urged to do it for the good of our little newborn community. I am deeply convinced that a new institute requires more care than an older one. I have always trusted that the help of a chaplain was near; but I have learned that, most probably, we will not have one this year; this news was a great blow to my courage. I fear, and with reason, that if we spend the year as we are, it will be impossible to employ any sisters in the schools next year; they will not be sufficiently trained, especially for catechism."[16]

Esther Blondin was aware that a well-rounded formation for the sisters was part of the quality of their commitment.[17] She considered this to be the most elementary form of justice. The book of the first rules of the community contained the following regulations written by hand: "Study is a strict duty for each sister (...) All should prepare themselves to serve in the various assignments of the community especially those dealing with edu-

---

[15] *Positio,* p. 476.

[16] *The Correspondence of Mother Marie Anne,* Letter to Bishop Bourget, December 16, 1850, p. 20.

[17] This explains certain prescriptions found in the community regulations, such as the daily study of the multiplication tables and the conjugation of verbs. See Sister Marie Jean de Pathmos, S.S.A., *Dossier sur la vie et les vertus,* p. 70. Though brief, this formation was adapted to the needs of the sisters and suited to the requirements of their work at that time.

cation. Let them be mindful that if children should lose their time, due to their ignorance, not only would the community be disgraced, but also, in justice, tuition should be refunded. They will devote themselves to study with method and application, ever mindful of the glory of God and the salvation of souls."[18] These twin motives sustained the foundress in her commitment and were the mainstay of her daily actions. Esther added to these motives that of "the good of the community", an expression she often wrote. There was nothing possessive in her attitude to the work she was undertaking; on the contrary, her perception of the community was of its being called forth by the Spirit of prophecy for efficacious action. By "the good of the community," Esther understood the achievement of that for which it was born; that is, the promotion of the rights of poor children and young people to an education. At that time, this idea was expressed as the zeal to instruct the children who were the poorest and the most deprived.[19]

From 1850 to 1853, Esther Blondin prepared her sisters for the task. She worked for the unity and the common good of the group.[20] She also sought to provide her community with a minimum of security.[21] In writing about the eventual purchase of some new land, an urgent need in Vaudreuil, she said: "There is a proposal to hold another (parish) meeting Sunday... Supposing the inhabitants, by dint of petition, were to grant us the land of the parish, if we have no access to the little river, we would stay there with no hope of enlarging if the need arose. In perpetual constraint, we would be hard put to carry out our proj-

---

[18] *The First Rules of the Sisters of Saint Anne,* Ninth Rule: Study, p. 58.

[19] See *Ibid.,* p. 59.

[20] One of Esther's first companions recalled the atmosphere of the community at that time, "We loved each other like sisters, sharing our joys and sorrows... This mutual support made us happy." See Sister Marie Jean de Pathmos, S.S.A., *Dossier sur la vie et les vertus,* p. 93.

[21] Financially, the community was in difficulty, and would remain so for a long time. Revenue from the students was too limited, and not much was required of new candidates. For these reasons, the sisters made hosts and candles, did sewing, cultivated a piece of land, and managed a bakery, barely to make ends meet. See *Ibid.,* p. 63.

ect.''[22] It had become necessary either to enlarge the convent-school or to build a house large enough to fill the needs of the young community that was experiencing rapid growth.[23] The Bishop of Montreal found another solution to this housing crisis. He decided to transfer the community to St. Jacques de l'Achigan, about 120 kilometers from Vaudreuil. The Madams of the Sacred Heart, who ran a school there, had decided to establish themselves closer to Montreal. Esther and her companions arrived there on August 23, 1853. Starting in October, always penniless, the foundress welcomed children for a new school year.[24]

So Esther Blondin's project was expanding. A sign of its real vitality was, for example, a request on June 21, 1852, by Archbishop François Norbert Blanchet, of Oregon City. He was visiting the young community and asked them to come to his diocese and teach the Aboriginal and Metis children. This appeal struck a chord in the heart of the foundress[25], at a time when no other community of women had yet penetrated the Canadian West. Though circumstances forced a negative reply to the request, still, Esther kept a lively desire to go to the West Coast some day and to send her sisters there. So, in concrete terms, this is how Esther perceived her mission as foundress, free to go where the Spirit led the way. Bishop Bourget, on a rare occasion when he wrote words of approval to her spoke of a "work so well begun."[26]

---

[22] *The Correspondence of Mother Marie Anne,* Letter to Bishop Bourget, April 25, 1853, p. 54.

[23] Given this situation, the number of boarders gradually diminished to seven or eight. Since their board constituted the principal source of revenue for the house, the financial problems this created become obvious.

[24] See *The Correspondence of Mother Marie Anne,* Letter to Bishop Bourget, October 4, 1853, p. 73.

[25] See *Positio,* p. 467, and Sister Marie Jean de Pathmos, S.S.A., *A History of the Sisters of Saint Anne,* p. 134.

[26] *The Correspondence of Mother Marie Anne,* Letter from Bishop Bourget, October 10, 1853, p. 74.

# The Winds of Contradiction

But major difficulties arose in St. Jacques that revolved around Louis Adolphe Delphis Maréchal,[27] the chaplain of the newly-established motherhouse. From that time, Esther Blondin's letters to the Bishop of Montreal expressed a growing anxiety in the face of the interfering ways of the newcomer. He took it upon himself, during her absence, to raise the children's tuition and to rent a house for the boarders, in the name of the Sisters of Saint Anne.[28] The bishop's surprising answer only complicated a troublesome matter: "Changing the fee for board and lodging without consulting you is an irregularity. I counsel you, nevertheless, to close your eyes to it while waiting further instructions. Be satisfied, for the moment, to answer nothing on the subject, just as if you knew absolutely nothing about it."[29] This tangled state of affairs turned out to be very painful for the foundress, who bore the burden of responsibility for her community.

[27] Father Louis Adolphe Delphis Maréchal was born on January 23, 1824. So he was 29 years old. Since his ordination on November 5, 1848, he had held six different posts, where he gave fully of his energy and his devotedness. He asked Bishop Bourget for the chaplaincy of the Daughters of Saint Anne, and had arrived at St. Jacques shortly after the sisters. The pastor of the parish already knew him, having once been his vicar (March 7, 1849-November 10, 1850). He wrote of him, "He has caused me much suffering, the dear child. He sowed discord all along my path." Maréchal was domineering, touchy, and tactless, but he certainly had good intentions. And, if he seemed like an evil force in Esther Blondin's life, the positive aspects of his influence must be recognized. He directed several young women towards the new community; he spent himself for the spiritual formation of the sisters; and he contributed to the pedagogic development of the community by teaching French and Arithmetic to the sisters. He also visited classes and the schools. Finally, he took to heart the financial interests of the community using his influence to obtain aid and to guarantee loans, which was no mean advantage, considering the indigence of the community at its outset. See Sister Marie Jean de Pathmos, S.S.A., *Dossier sur la vie et les vertus,* pp. 105, 151-157, 486-487, and *Mother Marie Anne, Foundress of the Sisters of Saint Anne,* translated by Sister Mary Camilla, S.S.A., from Eugène Nadeau's book *Martyre du silence,* p. 88.

[28] See *The Correspondence of Mother Marie Anne,* Letter to Bishop Bourget, October 12, 1853, pp. 78-84.

[29] *Ibid.,* Letter from Bishop Bourget, October 19, 1853, p. 77.

The whole situation deteriorated rapidly when the chaplain involved himself in the admission of sisters to religious profession, meddled in the daily life of the community and began to abuse his power as the sisters' confessor. On this latter point, Esther acted from conviction and fought to safeguard the freedom of conscience of her sisters. This led to a gradual loss of the bishop's trust that he had always shown towards her. She wrote to him in December 1853: "Father Chaplain, in leaving for his retreat, had recommended that the sisters not go to confession until his return. I do not know for what reason. But I did not believe it necessary to leave the sisters ten days without going to confession because Father Chaplain was absent. The next day... I asked (Father Romuald Paré, pastor and ecclesiastical superior of the community) if he would be kind enough to hear the sisters' confessions, or to send someone else if he deemed it advisable; but he came himself. I was glad to have such a timely opportunity to provide an extraordinary confessor for the sisters, because many of them were very strained with their confessor, to the point of making the confessions doubtful."[30] The bishop answered the letter in these terse words: "The chaplain is the representative of Jesus Christ. Go to him then in all simplicity and openness (...) You have to do great violence to yourself to speak to him. This trial is necessary (...) Be very discreet, also, so as to say nothing that might compromise you. Everything is repeated; it is hard to understand."[31] Incomprehensible indeed! Esther had to govern her community. She was expected to bring her ship through the stormy sea safely to port. Yet, she had the helm taken away from her.

The chaplain's schemes and the more or less tacit support he received from his bishop for many months, undermined Esther's influence and destroyed the unity of the sisters. The conflict became critical. And, while the foundress kept her discretion in the matter of her rights, Father Maréchal redoubled his outspokenness on the matter. Two of his letters to Bishop Bourget

---

[30] *Ibid.*, Letter to Bishop Bourget, December 12, 1853, p. 79.

[31] *Ibid.*, Letter from Bishop Bourget, December 20, 1853, p. 85.

influenced the turn of events. On June 10, 1854, he wrote, "Things are going very badly with the superior. She has never liked me and she will never get used to me — there will never be enough harmony between us to accomplish the desired good. I cannot believe that that girl is fit to form religious." Then on the following August 15, his attack was decisive: "I can tell you, my Lord, that you do not treat your servants as I have been treated in this house — I cannot hold on much longer — the superior wishes to change confessors — I beg you to consider the matter — you would not hurt my feelings, my Lord, if you gave me another position." [32] Three days later, the bishop called upon Esther Blondin to give in her resignation. The mission of the foundress seemed to have been definitively frustrated, unless she could hope for a complete turn of events. History shows that that would have been a vain hope.

## The Way of Faithfulness

While still in shock from such a severe jolt, Esther obeyed the bishop. There was no question here of justice, or clarification of areas of responsibility, or respect for all those involved, or even of frank dialogue. The foundress forgave Father Maréchal for the personal harm he had done to her, and especially, as she says so well, for the harm he had caused her community. Thus, she reacted in perfect fidelity to her gift of prophecy, seeing in these tragic events, the precious pearl to be safeguarded. It was the solidarity that bound her and her sisters in a common mission to the most needy, entrusted to them by God. And it was this keen sense of her mission that would lead her from then on, but not in the direction she had expected.

The years that followed her resignation found Esther at work, first as directress of the convent-school in St. Genevieve. Here,

---

[32] *Dossier sur la vie et les vertus,* Letters from Father Louis Adolphe Maréchal to Bishop Bourget, June 10, 1854, and August 15, 1854, pp. 202-203 and 210.

as at Vaudreuil and at St. Jacques, she kept her aim prophetic. Even though she was responsible for a school and a small community, she could still be found performing simple tasks in the service of the children and youth she was educating. She kept for herself the catechism class (as it was then called). "This teaching she gave not only to the convent pupils, but also to boys of sixteen and seventeen, who because of having to earn their living, had not been able to prepare for their First Communion."[33]

She was particularly sensitive to the needs of the sisters who shared her mission. The local doctor who saw her taking care of a Sister who was ill had this to say as testimony, "I never could have believed it, had I not seen it with my own eyes, how much the sisters love one another in religious communities."[34] And, as always, where the good of people was in question, the foundress let the Spirit lead her beyond the monastic rules of the day that applied to all forms of religious life. She wrote to her superior: "I must say that from Christmas Eve until today, we kept silence only on the first day; here are the reasons. The first is that Sister Marie Michel was suffering in two ways, physically and morally; on the first day of silence, she only cried the whole day, which was very bad for her headaches; since she could not talk alone, I gave recreation. The second reason is that spending most of our time in church the last days, we talked during the few moments we could get together."[35]

She acted just as freely, with complete disregard for her own reputation, where there was a question of justice towards those in her charge. Now, in the precarious position of the convent-school which she administered, she had fewer occasions for misunderstandings with authority because Father Maréchal interfered constantly. But, when her superior reproached her with not

---

[33] *Positio,* p. 396.

[34] Sister Marie Jean de Pathmos, S.S.A., *Dossier sur la vie et les vertus,* p. 317.

[35] *The Correspondence of Mother Marie Anne,* Letter to Mother Marie de la Purification, General Superior, January 5, 1858, p. 137.

sending enough financial help to the motherhouse and told her to cut back on food expenses, she replied: "As to what you recommended to me with regard to food for the sisters and pupils, I cannot conform to it without compromising one of my principal duties, without the risk of committing an injustice to the parish, and without failing in charity towards my sisters and the pupils. As for myself, I will conform in everything to your orders."[36] Taking such a stand was guaranteed to displease. Besides, the directress had taken steps to obtain government funds of one crown a month and a cord of wood for the winter.[37]

## The Deepening of a Mission

Within the limits that were imposed on her, Esther Blondin's prophetic mission became more and more interiorized. It was at this time that she promised to recite every day the Little Office of Saint Anne. Why did she do this? She did it to obtain for her daughters union of hearts and spirits in their search for the glory of God and the service of the most needy people. She committed herself to do this just as her life fell more and more into obscurity.

A significant even in 1857, however, revealed how Esther was always aware of her mission. She spontaneously volunteered to go to Vancouver Island, where the community had just accepted to open a new house.[38] She confided to Bishop Bourget that among the motives that guided her was "the desire which God placed in my heart to establish in this foreign land a motherhouse of our Institute, which later could send out missionaries around it."[39] No, the foundress was not finished, even though she had been reduced to performing unobtrusive tasks. "Let us offer our

---

[36] *Ibid.,* Letter to Mother Marie Angèle, General Superior, January 28, 1856, p. 111.

[37] See *Positio,* p. 397.

[38] At the request of Bishop Modeste Demers, Bishop of Vancouver Island.

[39] *The Correspondence of Mother Marie Anne,* Letter to Bishop Bourget, December 23, 1857, pp. 134-135.

sacrifices (...) since we cannot be great missionaries," she used to say after her offer had been refused.[40]

It was against this backdrop that she experienced a second dismissal. It was Father Maréchal who was actively and successfully involved on this occasion. Esther was recalled to the mother-house in the summer of 1858, because of her alleged incompetence to administer the convent-school at St. Genevieve. She began the thirty-two years of silence imposed on her, conscious of being at the root of a tree which nourished itself on her flesh and blood. At St. Jacques in the following years, she performed one manual task after another whether as dressmaker for the sisters, or as parish sacristan. On October 17, 1864, she was named to Lachine. She was fifty-five years old and was appointed to the sewing room, the care of the sick children, and the First Communion catechism class. Later, she served in the pharmacy, and the convent ironing room. Now, this last task placed her for more than twenty years in direct contact with entire generations of novices. The foundress carried out her mission to them no longer by word, by her own daring initiative or by her leadership, but by her silent influence.

In the community where she was no longer recognized, Esther continued to be present to her sisters. Her contemporaries said that every summer she was "happy to greet the dear missionaries who returned to the motherhouse for their retreat." She questioned them with interest about their health, their occupations, the progress of their classes, congratulating and encouraging them. "In her company", they said, "we spent many refreshing hours."[41] When distance separated her from her sisters, she wrote to them. This is what she wrote to the superior of St. Cuthbert: "Every day, and many times a day, I make it my duty to pray for all my dear missionary sisters. Certainly, it would please me very much to go to see you... Nevertheless, I very willingly offer the sacrifice to God, all the while, though,

---

[40] *Positio,* p. 404.

[41] *Ibid.,* p. 592.

giving myself the privilege of visiting you every day in spirit."[42] Right to the very end, the accomplishments of her sisters struck a chord in her heart. At age 70, she wrote to a sister in Nanaimo, B.C., "Dear little Sister, if I were permitted to envy another's happiness, I would envy yours. How fortunate I find you to work for the Glory of God by making Him known to dear children."[43]

There where she seemed to have been reduced to powerlessness, on so many misleading roads, the foundress recognized and silently confirmed the commitment of her sisters. And the prophetic character of her mission took on a whole new dimension.

## The Consistent Behaviour of the Prophets

### MOHANDAS GANDHI

Many prophets experience, as Esther Blondin did, an irresistible impulse to go ahead despite obstacles often considered insurmountable. Mohandas Gandhi, for example, left his law practice and opened an *ashram,* where he lived with his family. First he exchanged his European clothing for a cotton garb which he made himself. He led India into the spinning wheel revolution to achieve independence and economic recovery for his people. The *Mahatma* founded a periodical to spread his ideas, the *Young India,* in 1919; then, when the government suspended it as subversive, *The Haryian.*

Using symbolic actions, Gandhi gathered the crowds, focused their purpose and stirred their hearts. A case in point was the famous Salt March. In one of his biographies we read: "With a shrewd eye for maximum dramatic impact, he would march

---

[42] *The Correspondence of Mother Marie Anne,* Letter to Sister Marie Adrienne, December, 1889, p. 224.

[43] *Ibid.,* Letter to Sister Marie Théodore, September 27, 1879, p. 210.

from the *ashram* — slowly, very slowly — to the sea, a distance of 241 miles, with a group of followers (...) On foot, he and his people would march to the coastal town of Dandi (...) there he would scoop salt water from the sea and make salt."[44] This simple, transparent gesture electrified India and constituted a real challenge to the English colonies who claimed exclusive right to the salt. Later, the *Mahatma* noted: "Whatever striking things I have done in life, I have not done prompted by reason but prompted by instinct — I would say God. Take the Dandi Salt march of 1930 (...) Like a flash it came, and as you know, it was enough to shake the country from one end to the other."[45]

He was not satisfied, however, just to shake the burden of colonialism; Mohandas Gandhi next undertook the long struggle for the rights of the untouchables, the outcasts, who were victims of segregation throughout the whole of India. He gave the untouchables the name *haryians*; that is, sons of God. He preached by example. At home he did the menial tasks only the untouchables did and he received into his *ashram* a family of untouchables. Following a number of fasts and a round of activities to help them, he finally succeeded in shaking the age-old mentality that labelled them pariahs. From then on temples, roads, and public fountains opened up to them. Hindu children shared desks with them at school, and adults mingled with them in public eating places. Petitions and statements were circulated and mixed marriages took place. But, in this kind of revolution, psychological, religious and social, there was much suffering.

So it was for his commitment against what he called the vivisection of his country into two dominions, one Hindu, the other Moslem. No one knows how many steps Gandhi undertook nor how much anguish he suffered over this cause so dear to his heart. Even though at the end of his life he had the ear of all India, still he did not succeed in obtaining the unity of his country. On the contrary, on the 15th of August, 1947, two countries, India and Pakistan, were born from the newly-gained independence.

---

[44] Gerald Gold, *Gandhi a Pictorial Biography,* p. 85.
[45] Louis Fisher, *The Life of Mahatma Gandhi,* pp. 302-303.

He was disconcerted, but he did not give up. Until his violent death, he pursued his mission of justice and brotherly love, convinced that he was working with God.

## MARTIN LUTHER KING

Nearer to our own time, Martin Luther King struggled to free the blacks of the United States from segregation. He pursued his prophetic mission with daring. At the age of 26, he made his first move knowing that the task was greater than himself. With his black brothers and sisters from Montgomery, he organized a boycott of the public buses, where racism had become intolerable. Thousands of blacks walked daily to their work for 382 days and their nonviolent resistance succeeded in overcoming the segregation.

Martin Luther King had the genius to adapt Gandhi's methods to his Christian faith and to North America. He started a movement over which he presided and he enlisted courageous people whose collaboration was invaluable to him. Together, they adapted their activity more and more to the needs of a given area. Where black civil rights were trampled, where their right to vote was still denied, where social integration was closed to them, King and his movement formed, among other groups, the North Carolinians and helped them to organize themselves. They planned huge marches, sit-ins, and demonstrations in several American cities. In 1957 alone, the Baptist Minister delivered 208 allocutions and travelled 1,250,000 kilometers, all the while writing his first book *Stride Toward Freedom*. [46] He personally met three Presidents: Dwight David Eisenhower, John Fitzgerald Kennedy, and Lyndon Baines Johnson, to obtain official recognition of black civil rights. There were many dark hours for the prophet, but he continued to promote the fundamental rights and dignity of his own people.

He firmly believed that "there are some things in our world

---

[46] See Lerone Bennett, *What Manner of Man,* p. 96.

to which men of goodwill must be maladjusted."[47] That was why he urged his brothers and sisters to peaceful involvement and sacrifice of their social positions: "The Negro professional does not ask 'What will happen to my secure position, my middle class status, or my personal safety, if I participate in the movement to end the system of segregation?' but, 'What will happen to the cause of justice and the masses of Negro people (...) if I do not participate actively and courageously in the movement?'"[48] King preached by example. In 1965, he moved with his family to the slums of Chicago to share the lot of other blacks. The Nobel prize which he had won at that time, was worth $54,000 and he gave the whole sum to four associations that worked for the same causes he did. He acted times without number for his mission; and the same can be said of all the prophets.

Nevertheless, Martin Luther King was shaken by the violent turn the black revolution had taken in New York in 1964. "I condemn the violence of the riots; but I understand the conditions that cause them."[49] So, he decided to set in motion a new social program to counter the disastrous economic conditions of blacks which inflamed such extreme reactions. The Poor People's Campaign was impeded by the war in Vietnam, which exhausted social program funds. Though thoroughly disgusted by the politics of the Johnson Government, King, nevertheless, did not give up. His battle brought him into association with the international pacifist movement. He knew what was at stake; because in his eyes, only justice and peace could open the doors to any brotherhood worthy of the name.

## HÉLDER CÂMARA

Hélder Câmara, though in a different situation, walked in the steps of the prophets. From the beginning of his episcopate,

---

[47] Martin Luther King, *Strength to Love,* p. 14.

[48] *Ibid.,* p. 20.

[49] Coretta Scott King, *My Life with Martin Luther King, Jr.,* p. 297.

he performed personal deeds of sharing in the name of justice, all signs of the stand he was taking: He sold his episcopal insignia; he moved into a very simple house; he lived a frugal life; and he travelled often on foot carrying his briefcase. He had contact with the ordinary people on the street, and he opened the offices of the archdiocese to all comers.

His words matched his actions and they proved infectious in his diocese. He kindled the fire when he singled out areas of injustice. Hélder said of himself that when he fed the poor he was called a saint; but that when he asked why the poor had nothing to eat, he was called a communist.[50]

His commitment was already complicated, but it took on a whole new meaning at the Second Vatican Council. The Brazilian bishop discovered the worldwide dimensions and causes of underdevelopment. From that moment, he was more forceful in his denunciation of socio-economic structures and the postures which widened the gap between the rich countries and Third World countries. His word alone was action.

The dynamism of the bishop was again the source of a diocesan pastoral letter on the promotion of justice and of human rights. After some years, his influence spread beyond his own country, and he regularly accepted invitations to other countries. Everywhere he roused public opinion and prompted people to become involved in building a more humane society, according to the desire of God.

Because they were a threat, the positions he took caused him many contradictions, as they did to all the prophets. The Brazilian government cleverly ostracized him for more than ten years. Despite much repression, which made him like Esther Blondin, Dom Hélder Câmara pursued his mission through his episcopal duty of "conscientizing" all those with whom he came in contact. And he communicated this passion for peace and justice to thousands of the young and the militant throughout the world.

---

[50] See Dom Hélder Câmara quoted in *A Time to Speak Out,* p. 57.

# OSCAR ROMERO

His confrère, Oscar Romero, was going in a similar direction; especially during the three years that he was Archbishop of San Salvador. Faced with the social injustice and the violence of which he was a daily witness in his diocese, he finally took a stand. He used a private radio station, YSAX, to broadcast his views to the people of his diocese, "We know the danger that threatens our poor radio station for being an instrument of truth and justice, but we know the risk must be taken, because an entire people depend on it as they strive to uphold this word of truth and justice."[51]

His pastoral style brought him close to several prophets, and to Esther Blondin in particular, because his words educated people, made them conscious of a reality, and brought them together. Most of the time, his radio broadcasts took the form of weekly homilies to the country and to the neighbouring regions. The bishop went beyond vague comments on liturgical texts. He gave news of the various Christian communities; he identified, with particulars, all violations of human rights and acts of violence against peasants, families, committed Christians and their priests. Inspired by the Gospel and urged on by his mission, he took the lead in a situation that was becoming increasingly dark.

The prophet did not back away from his opponents nor from their threats. He continued to speak out and to write in the diocesan review, *Orientacion,* and he openly visited communities suffering from real persecution. Despite the lack of understanding and the denigration within the Church, he avoided actions that might jeopardize his commitment to the oppressed. For example, one of his biographers relates the following: "It was to celebrate the 'coronation' that Archbishop Gerada invited Romero to the nunciature. Romero replied by letter that, in spite of his fidelity and love for the Pope, he could not attend the reception that the nuncio was giving. 'Unfortunately, the publicity given

---

[51] Oscar Romero, *A Martyr's Message of Hope, Six Homilies by Archbishop Oscar Romero,* p. 116.

to these acts is eagerly used to give the public an image of the relations between the government and our local hierarchy that, in my opinion, make us bishops lose trust and credibility with our people, to whom we are chiefly committed."[52] His mission led him that far.

Oscar Romero was in contact with the masses of poor people, and in solidarity with his clergy and the people of his diocese. As a result, he made some discoveries about justice and peace. These could be achieved only through dynamic conscientization and organization of the public sector.[53] There had to be action powerful enough to put pressure on the public authorities. So, with that end in mind, he became so effective that he became a real threat to the authorities of Salvador...

That is what prophets are like! Their mission is essentially active, forged from their experience of God and their direct contact with reality. Their commitment, which brings them sufferings and difficulties, proves to be both creative and persevering in the face of the temptation to turn back. These common traits, which unite them, underscore the profound relationship of their beings. What could be said of Esther Blondin could easily be said of them all: "Be careful in dealing with a man (or a woman) who cares nothing for sensual pleasures, nothing for comfort or praise or promotion, but is simply determined to do what he believes to be right. He (or she) is a dangerous and uncomfortable enemy."[54]

Those are prophets! Yes, that is how they become threats, and all the more so since their action is coupled with a coherent statement that leaves no room for ambiguity.

------

[52] James R. Brockman, *The Word Remains: A Life of Oscar Romero,* p. 131. Henceforth, reference to this work will be made by the first half of this title, only.

[53] See Oscar Romero, *Assassiné avec les pauvres,* p. 43.

[54] Louis Fisher, *The Life of Mahatma Gandhi,* p. 118.

# Chapter 2

# A Prophetic Way of Speaking

*As to what you recommend to me... I cannot conform to it... without the risk of committing an injustice.*

Esther Blondin

*The tendency of most is to adopt a view that is so ambiguous that it will include everything and so popular that it will include everybody.*

Martin Luther King

It is commonplace to hear that prophets are men and women who speak out. There is good reason for this; yet, to confine their role only to the spoken word would be to minimize, even to distort their mission. Rather, the latter so absorbs their whole attention and is so global, that it gives unity to their entire lives. Their word cannot really be separated either from their behaviour or from their experience. There is a genuine human quality to their prophecy that is transparent. Before being men and women who speak out, they are men and women whose word is true. That is why they dare to enlighten their contemporaries, to appeal to them, and to denounce their deeds of injustice.

## The Honest Word

Esther Blondin's life bears abundant witness to the fact that she possessed that virtue of prophets, fidelity to her word. Even before her foundation at Vaudreuil, she was a woman of her word. She knew her plan was daring, not to mention illegal; yet, at the risk of incurring the disapproval of her pastor and the bishop, she was straightforward about her project. She kept this straight course throughout her life, at whatever the cost to herself. In 1852, as superior of the new community, she informed Bishop Bourget of some community problems she was experiencing. Others might have judged it better to remain silent about the matter. There was nothing to enhance the reputation of the foundress in disclosing it. Never mind that! Esther spoke freely about what was going on among her sisters, without being downcast or having a false sense of guilt. Nor was she motivated by a vain desire for success: "Sister Marie de l'Assomption twists our holy rules around and makes them unrecognizable... I was obliged to forbid her to have her sisters do work that could have harmed their health; she replied that she would do it again, that it was all sisters' tales. All the time that Sister Marie Joseph was there, she did her best to discourage her (...) I am inclined to believe (...) that the poor sister has lost her mind and that it would be more prudent to withdraw her from there. And I have given only a sketchy account of the miseries of the community."[1]

This singlemindedness was combined with great honesty when Esther gave an account of her own actions. In September 1853, she communicated to her bishop how she had received the new chaplain of St. Jacques: "I feel obliged to inform Your Grace of the reception I accorded Reverend Father Maréchal who announced himself on Sunday evening as chaplain of our community. I replied that I had received no letter from Your Grace announcing him as such: but, that it was in truth Reverend Father Barrette who is recognized as chaplain and announced as such by Your Grace's last letter dated August 17 and that we could not receive another without an order from you. My Lord, if in this I have committed an error, I beg Your Grace to forgive me; but I must tell you, that under the circumstances, I did not feel I ought to act otherwise. Allow me, Your Grace, to tell you in all confidence what I think is best for our community."[2] She did not distort the truth, but faced with the exigencies of her mission, the foundress was straightforward.[3]

---

[1] *The Correspondence of Mother Marie Anne,* Letter to Bishop Bourget, December 7, 1852, pp. 44-45. The religious in question was Suzanne Pineault, the one who had invited Esther to come and work with her at the school in Vaudreuil, about twenty years before.

[2] *Ibid.,* Letter to Bishop Bourget, September 4, 1853, p. 69.

[3] The foundress was telling the truth. She had received a letter from her bishop, who spoke to her about Father Louis de Gonzague Barrette as chaplain. The latter had gone to meet the community after his recent move to St. Jacques. There had been rumours about a possible change of the appointment she so appreciated. She wrote her thoughts on the affair to Bishop Bourget on August 27, 1853. She was quite aware of the unfavourable opinion the pastor, Father Paré had about his former assistant, Father Maréchal. The latter had delayed his visit to the convent, though he had arrived at St. Jacques some days before. In a situation surrounded by doubt, the foundress had,

She showed the same honesty, when she was dismissed from office, as directress of the St. Genevieve boarding school. She worked to protect the good of her sisters and she explained her conduct to her superior. The foundress had been reprimanded for not sending enough financial aid to the motherhouse: "You pointed out to me that the mission of Vaudreuil last year paid into the community treasury forty-seven louis. Allow me on this subject to make my own respectful observations (...) You say that with the profit we make from the tertiary boarders[4] I could have fed the sisters; the poor sisters, they would have had reason to complain if they had had only that much to eat."[5] Her words are striking both by the accuracy of her reasoning and the directness of her expression. Many other words of hers are just as striking.

Esther compromised herself, also, by her frankness about her plans. With her, being trustworthy was a matter of conscience. Witness this letter of December 23, 1857, when she told the bishop of her desire to establish a motherhouse on Vancouver Island. At the end of the letter, after having mentioned the reasons for her request, she revealed to him the state of her health in these words: "My Lord, I want to do all things frankly and sincerely; I do not want to cloak anything but to make things known as they are, so that (...) I will have peace of mind. I do not want to be a burden on anyone, nor to disappoint the hopes of His Grace (...) I have almost constant rheumatism; but that does not prevent me from going about my ordinary occupations and sometimes doing quite hard work (...) I could scarcely do harder work (...) But, if God wants me there (...) that causes me no worry."[6] Esther Blondin expressed herself in transpar-

therefore, shown herself prudent in the concern she showed for the spiritual good of her community. See Sister Marie Jean de Pathmos, S.S.A., *Dossier sur la vie et les vertus,* pp. 150-155.

[4] These were boarders who paid a minimum sum for tuition but whose parents continued to feed them. This explains the insufficient revenue to the house.

[5] *The Correspondence of Mother Marie Anne,* Letter to Mother Marie Angèle, General Superior, January 28, 1856, pp. 110-111.

[6] *Ibid.,* Letter to Bishop Bourget, December 23, 1857, p. 135.

ently clear and consistent terms, where facts about her mission or her person were concerned.

She was just as loyal to her own feelings. She expressed her displeasure to Sister Marie Jeanne de Chantal, her former novice become general secretary. The letter had relayed to her, in a roundabout way, Father Maréchal's reprimands. The foundress saw through the subterfuge and her reply went straight to the point: "I am answering nothing to the other statements in your letter. I usually keep silence on that; all that I can tell you is that you are enriching me with your cast-offs. (...) You tell me not to buy anything; well then, tell me if I must sell the pigs we have, or if I am to let them die of hunger, or if I am going to buy what is needed to feed them."[7] In that same letter, she also gave her opinion of the directives received and on the change in the holy habit, which had given rise to experimentation in religious apparel: "I tell you frankly that I found it ridiculous, during the last trip I made to the city, to see three sisters of the same community all coifed differently... You changed the manner of wearing these hats without advising us; and now we are being accused of disobedience."[8] Her tone, so lacking in diplomacy, played against the foundress whose reputation had already been undermined. In the event of a second dismissal, which she foresaw, she wrote to the bishop about her contact with him. She felt she should keep her distance from him: "Your Grace urged me to communicate to you in writing what I would have liked to tell you by word of mouth. I will do so through a spirit of obedience for some things, but I cannot for everything (...) I reserve for another time several other things which I will be able to communicate in writing, but there are some which I do not think I can do, or ought to do."[9] One of her contemporaries said so well, "Her frankness and her honesty were such that we really believe she could not disguise her thoughts."[10]

---

[7] *Ibid.*, Letter to Sister Marie Jeanne de Chantal, February 1858, pp. 146-147.

[8] *Ibid.*, p. 146.

[9] *Ibid.*, Letter to Bishop Bourget, July 5, 1858, pp. 158-160.

[10] *Positio*, p. 507.

# The Compromising Language

She was equally exacting about the truth in painful circumstances. The Superior, Mother Marie de la Purification, had demanded from Esther the 25 louis (app. $120) she had received from the government for the St. Genevieve school. The directress informed her that she had the authorization of Bishop Bourget to spend the money. The bishop, however, who had given only verbal authorization, now said, "that he had set a condition for the use of this money."[11] Because of this misunderstanding, and at the risk of being further discredited, the foundress defended what she believed was the truth: "My Lord, I cannot hide the surprise you caused me, and the confusion into which you threw me, in telling me that Your Grace had placed as a condition to the permission you were granting me, the reimbursement of these 25 louis to the community. My Lord, I would not want to say that Your Grace is adding now that you made this condition; I would not even want to think it; but I can say, and truthfully, that I have not the slightest recollection of it. Certainly, if I had heard and understood that this permission was given to me only on this condition I would have made representations to Your Grace, because I well knew that the house was not in a position to make this repayment before the end of the year, and I do not know if it will be able to do so even then."[12]

Esther was just as straightforward when she was sixty and was sent to St. Genevieve to negotiate with Father Louis Marie

---

[11] The condition seemed to have originated with some reports and complaints to the Bishop of Montreal by St. Jacques, to the effect that the St. Genevieve mission was not giving its share of financial support for the motherhouse. However, we know that despite its precarious finances, the St. Genevieve mission had sent St. Jacques the sum of $225 for 1854-1856. See Sister Marie Jean de Pathmos, S.S.A., *Dossier sur la vie et les vertus,* pp. 334-335 and 373.

[12] *The Correspondence of Mother Marie Anne,* Letter to Bishop Bourget, February 22, 1858, p. 143. On the subject of this misunderstanding, we know that Father Lefaivre took a stand and that he, too, could not understand how the motherhouse wanted to appropriate the money that was supposed to be for the school.

Lefaivre. Her superiors had brought her out of the shadows temporarily to obtain from the pastor the direction of the hospice he was building. Father Lefaivre knew Esther Blondin very well and esteemed her highly. His hospice was to be for the care of the poor and the aged of his parish. Esther was given a sealed envelope, unaware of its contents. Following this incident she sent a report on her assignment: "Father Lefaivre was very surprised by my arrival in St. Genevieve; he could not stop saying, 'But what is she coming to do?' (...) I brought the conversation around to the main topic and gave him the letter which he opened and read, without saying a word. I tell you frankly that I was very surprised to see a sealed letter in this envelope; it made me very uncomfortable."[13] It was Esther Blondin's way to speak the truth to whomever it might concern.

This attitude gave her remarkable freedom to accomplish her mission during her whole lifetime. She was 75 years old when the general superior read the Decree of Approbation of the Congregation. Esther noted an error in it about the place of foundation. She rose and simply said in front of the assembled community, "Allow me, Mother, to point out an error in the decree; the community began in Vaudreuil, not in St. Jacques."[14] During her life, the error, far from being corrected, was spread to every convent. But Esther had kept to the end a discreet speech that was worthy of being believed.

---

[13] *Ibid.,* Letter to Mother Marie Jeanne de Chantal, General Superior, April 23, 1869, pp. 190-191.

[14] *Positio,* p. 451. The first dossier sent to Rome requesting the approbation of the community, was presented by Bishop Bourget himself, during his visit of 1862. It was this dossier that contained a historical error that was to be repeated on the official decree of 1884. It is difficult to imagine how the Bishop of Montreal mentioned St. Jacques instead of Vaudreuil, as the place of foundation, since he himself had presided at the ceremony of first vows, in Vaudreuil; and had read to the community, that very day, its Decree of Erection. There are no historical documents today to shed light on this error; but it does fit in with the lot handed to the foundress. See Sister Marie Jean de Pathmos, S.S.A., *Dossier sur la vie et les vertus,* pp. 446-447.

# The Reliable Word of the Prophets

## MARTIN LUTHER KING

Prophets down through the ages have always been men and women true to their word. They are not afraid of the truth and they share their lives freely. At the beginning of his fight for the abolition of racist laws, Martin Luther King felt that his mission was beyond him. He was explicit about his anguish, "I am here taking a stand for what I believe is right. But now I am afraid. The people are looking to me for leadership, and if I stand before them without strength and courage, they too will falter. I am at the end of my powers." [15] In the eleventh month of the boycott of buses, he learned that the authorities had declared his car pool illegal. He felt completely defeated; and he informed his people of this fact, even at the risk of ruining their superhuman efforts in this just and nonviolent cause. "When the evening came, I mustered sufficient courage to tell them the truth." [16]

Honesty characterized the great moments of Martin Luther King's struggle.. After President John F. Kennedy's death, he promised his support to the successor, Lyndon Johnson. King also warned the president that anti-racist demonstrations would continue without letup in the fight of his people for their rights. His strategy resembled Esther Blondin's. It was based on truth. Even though he was criticized by the White House, he was fearless in expressing his views. He told a journalist what he thought about the war in Vietnam. "I want you to know that this is a moral commitment with me, and I have had a great deal of anxiety over the fact that I haven't been able to take a position publicly earlier." [17] It was a clear statement that obviously constituted a threat to the status quo and to certain political interests.

---

[15] Martin Luther King, Jr., *Stride toward Freedom, The Montgomery Story*, p. 134.

[16] Id., *Strength to Love*, p. 50.

[17] Coretta Scott King, *My Life with Martin Luther King, Jr.*, pp. 295-296.

# MOHANDAS GANDHI

Mohandas Gandhi knew all about plain speaking. He declared in 1922: "The Viceroy, Lord Reading, must clearly understand that the noncooperators (those who disobey unjust civil laws) are at war with the government. The strength of a noncooperator lies in his going to jail uncomplainingly. This is a fight to the finish."[18] He avoided all intrigue from whatever source and went straight toward his goal. "Diplomacy was not his forte; he always spoke bluntly; and he had no patience with fools."[19] He wrote to the viceroy on March 2, 1930, to inform him of a new campaign of civil disobedience: "Dear friend, before embarking on civil disobedience and taking the risk I have dreaded to take all these years, I would fain approach you and find a way out. My personal faith is absolutely clear (...) While, therefore, I hold British rule to be a curse, I do not intend to harm a single Englishman (...) If people join me, as I expect they will, the sufferings they will undergo, unless the British nation retraces its steps first, will be enough to melt the stoniest hearts. This letter is not in any way intended as a threat but is a simple and sacred duty peremptory on a civil resister."[20] Mohandas Gandhi, as well as Esther Blondin and the other prophets, did not give way to either blackmail or deception.

He was especially honest in his dealings with the English. In 1941, there was a new proposal for the constitution. Gandhi foresaw future divisions that would lead to the destruction of national unity. He considered this too high a price to pay for the freedom of his country. The proposal gave independence to India, but allowed each province, each faction, to negotiate its own entente with Great Britain. The *Mahatma's* reaction, so sharp and so direct, gave an inkling of the magnitude of the disaster he expected. "My firm opinion is that the British should leave

---

[18] Gerald Gold, *Gandhi a Pictorial Biography,* p. 77.

[19] Robert Payne, *The Life and Death of Mahatma Gandhi,* p. 458.

[20] Gerald Gold, *Gandhi a Pictorial Biography,* pp. 82 and 85.

India now in an orderly manner."[21] Whether in negotiations or in his private life, Gandhi's word was unequivocal.

His honesty made him the equal of any person of any rank. In 1942, he wrote to the Viceroy, Lord Linlithgow: "I had almost despaired of ever hearing from you (...) Your letter gladdens me to find that I have not lost caste with you. My letter of December 31 was a growl against you. Yours is a counter-growl (...) Convince me that I was wrong and I will make ample amends."[22] Such was Gandhi, who described himself as a "searcher after truth."[23] Prophets are like that. They live life to the full every day as well as in the great combats where their mission leads them.

## HÉLDER CÂMARA

Hélder Câmara's life proves that he, too, spoke without compromising conscience. He was once asked if he were going to a communist country that wanted to give him a peace prize. He replied, "No, because I've always said I would never go anywhere that I wasn't sure I'd be able to speak with love and freedom and without having my words used for propaganda."[24] He was just as free when expressing his opinion. "You know, there are still people who think that the reason there are poor and rich is that that's the way God wanted it, or because there are lazy or inept races. It's ridiculous!"[25] Speaking clearly had its advantages. He could always respect points of view different from his own: "I know a great number of people who put more trust in arms than in active nonviolence in the struggle against injustice and oppression. I respect them when they make this choice in good conscience. With due respect for them I say that this is not my choice."[26]

---

[21] *Ibid.,* p. 115.

[22] Louis Fisher, *The Life of Mahatma Gandhi,* p. 387.

[23] *Ibid.,* p. 233.

[24] Hélder Câmara, *Questions for Living,* p. 44.

[25] *Ibid.,* p. 54.

[26] *Ibid.,* pp. 92-93.

He was also honest enough to recognize his own limitations. He often admitted to his inability to solve every question. "My friends will have to forgive me. Those are questions I carry with me in my heart, in my prayer. But they are questions that I cannot answer."[27] His incomprehension was manifest in the face of quarrels that broke out among groups of committed Christians. "I'm very familiar with these quarrels. We have them, too, since we're the ones with the Third World problems. But, I don't understand them."[28] He was just like Esther Blondin in that he was not trying to protect his self-image. He even told about having taken part in what he later considered the greatest error of his life: As a young priest, he had joined a party that was putting pressure on some political candidates to sponsor a programme... prepared by the Chruch.

He denounced his brother-bishops for their apparent pact with injustice, but he never condemned them. When he spoke, he often showed his concern for episcopal unity. Without sacrificing truth, he made use of his marvelous sense of humour. To the comment, "Here in France you find precious few bishops accused of communism. That must mean something," he replied, "It seems to me very simply that it's either because there aren't any bishop-accusers in France or because they're smarter than ours."[29] He respected people; therefore, he would change the slant of a sensitive question rather than reveal anyone's secret embarrassing truth. But he laughed easily about himself and told the truth about himself. "I appreciate the great distance between what I am saying and what those who hear me can see and recognize. Fortunately, there is the breath of God's Spirit!"[30]

[27] *Ibid.,* p. 39.
[28] *Ibid.,* p. 57.
[29] *Ibid.,* p. 38.
[30] *Ibid.,* p. 4.

# OSCAR ROMERO

The Spirit of truth also guided Oscar Romero. In his first interview as archbishop, he revealed what could be expected of him: "We must keep to the centre (...) but seeking justice (...) The government should not consider a priest who takes a stand for social justice as a politician or a subversive element when he is fulfilling his mission in the politics of the common good."[33] Till the end of his life his word became more and more committed, reliable and firm. He often refuted news items circulated by the government or its paramilitary organization. In his archdiocese, he established a special commission to seek out and publish the truth about secret police work. This involved cases of torture, disappearances, assassinations, defamation, and other acts of injustice. Several times he requested judicial inquiries and called on political leaders to make laws respecting human rights. Nevertheless, he once publicly stated, "We wish to believe in the verbal promises of the president (...) But unfortunately, these actions tend to contradict those promises."[32]

In the contention between himself and the nuncio, Romero was very straightforward in trying to reach an understanding with him. Reading about it is like reliving an episode in Esther Blondin's life. Denunciations poured in to Rome; consequently, the Archbishop of San Salvador was constrained to explain his relationship with the nuncio to Cardinal Sebastiano Baggio to whom he wrote: "With sadness I must manifest that in these circumstances (...) I have not had his support in my actions. On the contrary, at certain moments I have felt very hard his pressure against my decisions. On analyzing this strange attitude of his, I have concluded that he lives at a great distance from the problems of our clergy and of humble people and that with him what has most weight are the reports and pressures of Cardinal Casariego, of the politicians, of the diplomats, and of the moneyed

---

[31] James R. Brockman, *The Word Remains,* p. 4.
[32] *Ibid.,* p. 178.

class of the elegant neighbourhoods."[33] He showed the same honesty when he refused, on April 5, 1978, to sign the declaration written by his brother-bishops. It was published in the newspapers and it condemned priests and religious who questioned the conduct of the nuncio in collaborating with an oppressive power. Romero insisted on giving a hearing to those who were being condemned and to dialogue with them about the problem. He expressed his dissidence and explained his position to each of the bishops concerned and to the nuncio.

His correspondence with the Roman Congregations shows the same attitude of frankness. The contradictory reports about him to Cardinal Baggio made Romero's position very difficult. After a conversation with Baggio, he wrote to him: "From your invitation of May 16, I expected to hear 'the most contrary reports, both good and bad. Both of them, genuine and spontaneous...' But I am left with the impression that among the reports that you had in mind the negative ones prevailed almost exclusively and that my explanations or answers did not receive official backing."[34]

So there is a common trait that unites the prophets. Their language is credible and genuine. The life of each one is cohesive. This empowers them to be daring in speech because it is free of all flattery and equivocation. This word, this language, which is part of their mission, becomes a forceful means of exhortation and of denunciation. It helps them to build and to tear down, to plant and to uproot as the Bible says.

## The Word That Fosters Growth

It was this very aim that most often made Esther Blondin speak out. We know, for example, that she herself formed the first generation of her sisters while giving them religious instruction. She wrote to Bishop Bourget, "Five of my sisters are

---

[33] *Ibid.,* p. 64.
[34] *Ibid.,* p. 118.

admitted to investiture (...) I fear, and with reason, (...) that they will not be sufficiently trained, especially for catechism. I explain it to them every Sunday."[35] We know, also, that she gave them commentaries on the community rules, and that she made herself available for consultation with them on their spiritual life. "The sisters would like to have the freedom," she said to the bishop, "to see me during the retreat for direction (...) I am prepared to sacrifice the retreat to hear them."[36] Esther used the word "hear" advisedly, when it was a question of spiritual dialogue. She was trying to recognize the Spirit who was at work in each one.

Besides instructing and enlightening her sisters, the foundress comforted them, encouraged them and urged them on by her goodness and firmness. She remained faithful to this ministry which formed part of her mission even after her removal from office. In December 1856, she wrote to the Vaudreuil community: "Let us enter into God's plan for us; let us be what he wants us to be; that is, religious sincerely attached to our vocation (...) Let us be faithful in little things, and we will deserve to be so in the greater... Thus, God will be with us in time and we will be with Him in eternity."[37] In 1858, Esther wrote to her young superior, once her Vaudreuil novice, with all the respect due to her office: "May the Spirit of Wisdom be always with you and guide you in all your actions... Under your superiorship, may the little family of Saint Anne pass happy and tranquil days; may each of its members find in you a mother's heart which knows how to commiserate with each one's sorrows, to give justice to the innocent, and to recognize the guilty. May this Spirit of Wisdom close your ear to false reports, to detractions, to calumny and slander; may it be open only to hear those who speak the truth, and who tell only the truth."[38]

---

[35] *The Correspondence of Mother Marie Anne,* Letter to Bishop Bourget, December 16, 1850, p. 20.

[36] *Ibid.,* Letter to Bishop Bourget, August 4, 1854, p. 96.

[37] *Ibid.,* Letter to her sisters, December 26, 1856, pp. 118-119.

[38] *Ibid.,* Letter to Mother Marie de la Purification, General Superior, January 5, 1858, p. 136.

Several letters, that she wrote in her old age still had that spark which lit up hearts and encouraged the sisters to be their best selves. It was especially to the sisters in faraway missions that her letters had that ring: "Believe me, my dear Sister, that the distance which separates us does not dull my affection for a sister who devotes herself so generously for the glory of God and the salvation of souls; it is rather a new motive never to forget you."[39] The last letter she wrote just a few days before she died was to Sister Marie Adrienne. She was still alert. She still recognized her mission in the work the sisters were doing. She still animated those whom God sent to share her mission: "I was extremely comforted, (...) by all the good news you give me about your house; I rejoice over it before the Lord, and I am confident that God will continue to make your zeal fruitful and to bless your works. It could not be otherwise since your dear companions are one with you in working for the good of the souls of your dear pupils."[40]

## The Word That Rebukes

Esther Blondin often spoke out, then, to draw her sisters closer together and, as she herself said, to edify them. Her word also condemned evil, particularly the evil of injustice, and whatever threatened the unity and the good of her community. At the beginning of the foundation, for example, she voted against a council decision which she considered unjust towards future candidates. She gave an account of her position to Bishop Bourget: "In the admission of these subjects and the refusal of a few others, there is something that surprises me. A young lady of good family, with a gift for teaching, (...) competent in manual works, charming in manners, with a spirit of simplicity, of candour and admirable openness, able to pay all her expenses, was refused (...) there seems to be a sentiment of jealousy in some, and avarice in others.

---

[39] *Ibid.,* Letter to Sister Marie Joachim, July 2, 1876, p. 204.

[40] *Ibid.,* Letter to Sister Marie Adrienne, December 1889, p. 224.

They wanted to make her pay board in the novitiate; I opposed it, this not having been established. I do not agree that we should make this one pay more than the others, or that she should be prevented from entering."[41] Just after her dismissal from office, and while she was still under a cloud, the foundress wrote to the bishop. She was reminding him of the sisters' rights under the constitutions, rights which she felt were being violated: "All have well understood the right which the constitution gives them to re-elect the same person as many times as they think before God that it is for the good of the community; but they were very much surprised to see that Your Grace was taking from them the freedom to act according to the spirit of the constitutions in taking away the eligibility of one of their members."[42] We know that at St. Genevieve she insisted on providing for her sisters and the students decent, though frugal, living conditions. We know, too, how much pressure was exerted by the mother-house to get money from her. On that point, Esther reminded her superiors of the laws of justice.

From 1858 until her death, she became less vocal in her admonitions and spoke through her actions, occasionally accompanied by a discreet word. A novice was astonished to discover the foundress of the community in charge of the ironing room in the basement of the motherhouse. The foundress said, "Our Lord planted the root in manure; that's why the tree grew so fast."[43] If the sisters by their criticisms recalled the deep wounds caused by Father Maréchal in the community, she reprimanded them. One of her contemporaries said, "If anyone forgot herself on that point, she was corrected."[44] Nevertheless, Esther never denied the tragic reality. Beyond the events, it was her whole life which became a silent affirmation of truth and unity. During the thirty-two years of her seclusion, Esther Blondin's gift of prophecy expressed itself in no other way.

[41] *Ibid.,* Letter to Bishop Bourget, July 15, 1851, p. 31.
[42] *Ibid.,* Letter to Bishop Bourget, August 20, 1854, p. 99.
[43] *Positio,* p. 536.
[44] *Ibid.,* p. 593.

# The Fecundity and Challenge
# of the Prophetic Word

## MARTIN LUTHER KING

Martin Luther King was never silenced. That was not, however, because the Baptist Minister spoke less forcefully; or that he did nothing to bring about a better world. When he called his people together, he exhorted them to come out of the apathy and the passivity that imprisoned them: "The belief that God will do everything for man is as untenable as the belief that man can do everything for himself. It, too, is based on a lack of faith. We must learn that to expect God to do everything while we do nothing is not faith, but superstition."[45] During his struggle, he often spoke to those who had the power to effect change. "I believe there are several programs that can reverse the tide of social disintegration."[46] He realized that laws could secure the civil rights of blacks and that socio-economic programs could foster their complete integration into North America. He called on his people to "fashion new tactics (...) which serve (...) to compel unwilling authorities to yield to the mandates of justice,"[47] because he observed that the oppressors did not give up their "rights" and perpetuated the notion that the hour of freedom had not rung yet.

Martin Luther King was at the heart of the movement over which he presided. He attached great importance to the formation of its members. He directed this formation towards nonviolence, and the respect and dignity of persons. He held endless sessions, seminars, meetings. By his own word and his own conviction, he won over some of his brothers and sisters who had seen no other way out than by the law of violence. Esther Blondin had acted in the same way.

---

[45] Martin Luther King, *Strength to Love*, p. 123.

[46] Id., *The Trumpet of Conscience*, p. 13.

[47] *Ibid.*, p. 14.

The Baptist Minister denounced vehemently certain decisions made by people responsible for maintaining the status quo. "The President (Kennedy) has proposed a ten-year plan to put a man on the moon. We do not yet have a plan to put a Negro in the state legislature of Alabama."[48] He went so far as to call weak and hypocritical the members of the government's executive power. In the celebrated March on Washington where he spoke on August 23, 1963, his wife reported that "his main contention was that instead of honoring her sacred obligations, America has given the Negro a bad check." And he added, "We are here today to redeem that check, and we will not accept the idea that there is no money in the Bank of Justice."[49]

He vigorously condemned the war in Vietnam which he described as immoral and an enemy of the poor. To those who expressed surprise at the stand he took on international affairs, he showed that "justice is indivisible. It would be rather absurd to work passionately and unrelentingly for integrated schools and not be concerned about the survival of a world in which to be integrated."[50]

## MOHANDAS GANDHI

Martin Luther King was a disciple of Gandhi, in whose footsteps he followed. During the course of his long career, Gandhi often stirred the conscience of his people. One day in February 1916, he participated in the grandiose inaugural ceremony of a college of the University of Benares. He had been invited as one of the guest speakers. Before the princes and dignitaries, he spoke very bluntly: "Whenever I hear of a great palace rising in any great city of India (...) I become jealous at once and say, 'Oh, it is the money that has come from the agriculturalists'... There cannot be much spirit of self-government about us, if we take away or allow others to take away from the peasants almost the

---

[48] Lerone Bennett, *What Manner of Man,* p. 120.

[49] Coretta Scott King, *My Life with Martin Luther King, Jr.,* p. 239.

[50] Martin Luther King, *The Trumpet of Conscience,* p. 24.

whole of the results of their labour. Our salvation can only come through the farmer. Neither the lawyers, nor the doctors, nor the rich landlords are going to secure it. Congress beware!''[51] There was an uproar in the auditorium; while some of the princes left the hall, a few students shouted, ''Bravo!'' He was interrupted even before he had finished speaking; but he was unperturbed by the commotion he had provoked. The following year he joined the indigo farmers who were being unjustly treated. When the struggle intensified, an Englishman, a supporter and friend of Gandhi, offered his services to the group. Gandhi declined the offer and took the occasion to reprove his people for their weakness. ''You think that in this unequal fight it would be helpful to have an Englishman on our side. This shows the weakness of your heart. The cause is just and you must rely upon yourselves to win the battle.''[52]

Like Esther Blondin and so many of the prophets, the *Mahatma* was not gentle where justice was an issue. He castigated untouchability as a boycotting of human beings. In the same way he qualified the Hindu-Moslem rivalries as crimes against religion and against humanity. When he stood trial for his campaign of civil disobedience, he declared to the judge: ''I believe that I have rendered a service to India and England by showing in noncooperation the way out of the unnatural state in which both are living (...) Judge, your choice is either to resign your post, and thus disassociate yourself from evil, or inflict on me the severest penalty if you believe that the system and the law you are assisting to administer are good for the people of this country and that my activity is, therefore, injurious to the public weal.''[53] Mohandas Gandhi's denunciations went even beyond that statement, to calling into question those he respected and whom he called his friends.

---

[51] Louis Fisher, *The Life of Mahatma Gandhi,* p. 134.

[52] *Ibid.,* p. 154.

[53] Gerald Gold, *Gandhi a Pictorial Biography,* p. 77.

# HÉLDER CÂMARA

Dom Hélder Câmara understood his prophetic mission in the same way: "We have the right and the duty to sound all the warning we deem necessary; to make any accusations that should in good conscience be made; to encourage, propose... question men and speak to God. Our right to do this is rooted precisely in the conviction that what is at stake is the destiny of our people, our own flesh and blood."[54] First, he encouraged his own people to be leaders and to be discriminating in the choices they made. "Let us never retreat from the challenges of progress," he boldly proclaimed, (...) "Let us bear in mind that the only truly humane solutions to human problems lie along the road of progress... But let us be careful not to crush anyone, not to leave anyone lying in the ditch."[55] The Bishop of Recife often returned to this subject of progress. "It is not industrialization that is to blame, but the way people develop it."[56] Another time he said: "I often hear a consumer society condemned in your countries, as if it were shameful to consume! Not at all! What is shameful and scandalous is waste (...) Overconsumption not only wounds justice — it wounds good sense, intelligence, and sometimes even your health!"[57] The prophet was tireless in singling out selfishness as the cause of the discord that was so corrosive of human and international relationships.

He was energetic in his denouncement of what he called "internal colonialism, the system through which some Brazilians base their wealth on the misery of other Brazilians,"[58] and he made public what he considered to be "the gravest social problem of our our time... the widening gulf between the people who are becoming richer and the people who are becoming

---

[54] Hélder Câmara, *Revolution through Peace,* p. 143.
[55] Id., *Questions for Living,* p. 50.
[56] *Ibid.,* p. 51.
[57] *Ibid.,* p. 62.
[58] Id., *Revolution through Peace,* p. 144.

poorer."[59] He also identified the roots of the evil, "in the heart, the interests, and the practices of the rich countries, with the complicity of the rich in the poor countries."[60] At times, gripped by the urgency of the corners to be turned, his denunciations became threats: "Alas for those with no heart for the struggle, the satiated, those who have lost their hunger and thirst for justice. Alas for those who love their own lives and do not know how to lose them. Alas for those who cling to their reputations, honor and convenience."[61] In his view, war is a major folly that perpetuates underdevelopment. That kind of talk made allies, but it also made enemies; and it was just as much a part of the struggle of the prophets as were commitment and action.

## OSCAR ROMERO

It was Oscar Romero's way, also, to speak from faith and conviction. He was very good at persuading his people, and shaking their passivity. He called on his Salvadorean brothers and sisters, whom he cherished, to wake up to the fact that they were the builders of their country.[62] At the beginning of Lent in 1980, he publicly addressed the military. He appealed to them not to allow the oligarchy to continue using them to defend its interests. He challenged them to guarantee freedom of speech, of assembly, and of organization. He asked them to lend their support to bringing about much-needed changes in the country.[63]

In his numerous homilies, he indicated where he recognized the work of the Spirit of Christ. It was particularly at the funerals of committed Christians, whether lay, religious or priest, who had died because of their involvement in the struggle to

---

[59] *Ibid.*, p. 87.

[60] Id., *Questions for Living,* p. 60.

[61] Id., *Revolution through Peace,* p. 130.

[62] See Oscar Romero, *Assassiné avec les pauvres,* p. 43.

[63] See *Ibid.,* pp. 145-146.

bring about peace and justice; and so that the development of all peoples and of the whole person not have been a word spoken in vain by the Second Vatican Council.[64]

He combined denunciation with exhortation in his New Year's pastoral message in 1980. He declared that it was the structures of social injustice which crucified the poor of his country. It was these structures that condemned the poor to a slow death. He called them a radical denial of the God of the living.[65] When a fifth priest of his diocese was assassinated, Archbishop Romero publicly addressed the civil authorities. He thundered at them: "Where is justice in our country? Where is the Supreme Court? Where is the honour of our democracy if people are to die in this way like dogs, and their deaths left uninvestigated like that of Father Rafael? I ask and demand in the name of citizenry that this be investigated and that an end be brought to this growing spiral of violence."[66] He spoke with contempt about what he called the idolatry of wealth, of private property considered as an absolute in the capitalist system, of the idolatry of political power in the regimes of national security in which they institutionalize the insecurity of the individual.[67] In February 1980 he wrote to the president of the United States, Jimmy Carter, to warn him against any intervention that would limit the rights of the Latin-American people to self-determination.[68]

Oscar Romero often reminded people of his responsibility as shepherd. Esther Blondin might have said as much in her time... The mission he was given compelled him to speak, despite the tragic turn of events. The Archbishop of San Salvador still insisted in his last homily of March 23, 1980. "We have the duty of pointing out the realities, also, of seeing how God's plan is reflected among us or despised among us."[69]

---

[64] See *Ibid.,* p. 41.

[65] See *Ibid.,* p. 37.

[66] James R. Brockman, *The Word Remains,* p. 161.

[67] See Oscar Romero, *The Voice of the Voiceless,* p. 183.

[68] See Oscar Romero, "Letter to President Carter" in Placido Erdozain, *Archbishop Romero, Martyr of Salvador,* pp. 77-79.

[69] James R. Brockman, *The Word Remains,* p. 216.

Words at once so authentic and so challenging, so straight-forward and so involving are of themselves striking actions. The prophets who "bridge the gulf between practice and profession,"[70] as Martin Luther King said, care as little for their own popularity as they do for their fate. They literally become one with their mission. It is a perilous mission. Oscar Romero said, "He that accuses must be ready to be accused... but... there is no pride or ill will or distortion of what the Gospel bids me preach to this archdiocese that has been committed to me."[71]

---

[70] Martin Luther King, *Strength to Love,* p. 26.

[71] James R. Brockman, *The Word Remains,* p. 150.

# Chapter 3

# A Prophetic Destiny

*I remained zero all year.*

Esther Blondin

*The only true prophet is a dead one.*

Pierre Gilbert

Neutrality, diplomacy, intrigue, are all attitudes that are foreign to prophets. Their position on any issue is freely taken, it is clear and firm, and is often destabilizing to the traditional order. That is what prophets are like, and they soon discover who their enemies are. Perhaps that is why their destiny is a tragic one; it seems to be a mark of their mission. Jesus of Nazareth Himself experienced it; and His disciples, by remaining faithful, follow in His footsteps: "Blessed shall you be when men hate you, when they ostracize you and insult you and proscribe your name as evil because of the Son of Man. On the day they do so, rejoice and exult, for your reward shall be great in heaven. Thus it was that their fathers treated the prophets."[1]

## The Violence Intensified

Esther Blondin's destiny was inseparable from her mission as foundress, her prophetic mission. From the very beginning she met with resistance for her daring commitment from the clergy, the episcopate, and her own family. But her leadership, her truthful word, and her keen sense of justice became targets for Father Louis Adolphe Maréchal. He won Bishop Bourget over to his side, at least as far as events were concerned. The first act of this drama was all in one scene. Esther Blondin had written to her bishop to inform him of the manner in which she had received the new chaplain at St. Jacques. Bishop Bourget showed no regard for her prudence, her responsibility, or the concern she had for the good of her community. Rather, he blamed her and humiliated her unjustly. This reaction was just a prelude to

---

[1] Luke 6:22-23.

the attitude he would adopt towards her each time there was a conflict between herself and Father Maréchal.[2]

Less than four months after the event, relationships had deteriorated somewhat. In a letter to Bishop Bourget, Esther Blondin wrote: "I would not have wanted for all the world that such an occurrence as happened on the eleventh of this month would have happened in our little community (...) I was summoned on Sunday morning to the tribunal of two of my sisters to be accused in their presence and there, like a criminal before his judges, I kept a dismal silence all the while Father Chaplain spoke; it was he who played the role of accuser (...) I begged him several times to be good enough to let me speak; I could not obtain this favour; I had to keep silence. And then he vented his spleen (...) Father Chaplain is not pleased that I refuse to pay the rent on a house which he leased for the community to have board and lodging fees from the quarterly boarders, and that we refuse to heat this house. I spoke of it to Father Paré (ecclesiastical superior) and he does not want us to pay a single penny... I have been blamed for maintaining that the fee for board and lodging should not be changed. I am quoted as saying many things which I did not say, and those which I did say cannot be remembered any more (...) He told me that I told him he was doing evil in the house. Here is what I said to him, that the lack of understanding among the Father Superior, the chaplain, and the Sister Superior does much harm in a community (I believe this to be true) and that it caused me much heartache to see that we did not get along, that already several sisters had made the observation to me. These, my Lord, are all my crimes."[3] It was the divisions fracturing the community that touched the foundress so deeply. For months, the bishop had but one answer to this incident, and others like it. She must close her eyes, say nothing and let the matter drop.

---

[2] On the attitude of Bishop Bourget towards Esther Blondin, see Sister Marie Jean de Pathmos, S.S.A., *Dossier sur la vie et les vertus,* pp. 259-262.

[3] *The Correspondence of Mother Marie Anne,* Letter to Bishop Bourget, December 12, 1858, pp. 80-84.

This temporizing, which at best was equivocal, abetted Maréchal's increasing interference in the community and his denigration of the foundress.[4] The chaplain even held Esther responsible for the disunity that resulted among her sisters. His manipulation was so skillful that he obtained her dismissal scarcely a year after his arrival in St. Jacques.[5] Following this painful event, Esther Blondin became ill. During her stay in the infirmary, she received a letter from her bishop, suspecting her of spreading calumny about her own community: "It has come to my attention, indirectly, that fourteen sisters of your community are on the point of giving up their state. Mr. Toupin, with whom I know you keep correspondence, came to tell me this sad news yesterday (...) I made up my mind today to write a word to you about it (...) I believe you ought to work to dispel this false opinion (...) You know, there is no absolution for the one who, having stolen or calumniated, is unwilling to repair the injury done to her neighbour."[6] This time, the superior came to the defense of the foundress, but it was in vain. The bishop no longer put his trust in Esther Blondin.

Father Maréchal continued to malign her. In his letters, he labelled her as visionary, hypocrite, moonstruck, insane, conceited, scheming, deceitful.[7] He even insinuated that she was the

---

[4] Bishop Bourget's attitude towards Esther Blondin is astonishing. He seemed to withdraw from her, while at the same time he lent a benevolent ear to the suggestions and doings of the chaplain. In this regard, it is noteworthy that the tone of the bishop's letters to Esther changed, and that after 1853, there was no further expression of the warm trust he had shown her in the early days. See Sister Marie Jean de Pathmos, S.S.A., *Dossier sur la vie et les vertus,* pp. 163 and 170.

[5] Her dismissal seems to be linked to Bishop Bourget's withdrawal of his confidence in her, on the instigation of Father Maréchal. Or would the bishop simply want to assure the survival of the community by taking a stand in a situation that could not continue? The way in which the decision was made, however, can still be questioned. See Leon Pouliot, S.J., *Monseigneur Bourget et son temps,* III, p. 95.

[6] *The Correspondence of Mother Marie Anne,* Letter from Bishop Bourget, September 12, 1854, pp. 103-104.

[7] See *Positio,* Letters from Father Louis Adolphe Delphis Maréchal to Bishop Bourget, August 15, and September 16, 1854, p. 305.

sister of one Emilie Blondin, a woman well-known for being a visionary.[8] A few of the sisters knew of this opinion of his, and of his determination to have the foundress expelled from the community. He imposed silence on them under pain of sin. He wrote to Mother Marie Angèle, the new general superior, "You ask yourself why I hold so strongly to your Mother being expelled from the community (...) In giving her this counsel, I have no more antipathy towards her than towards anyone else."[9] There was, therefore, a serious accusation charged against the foundress, who obviously could not defend herself, being sick in the infirmary since her dismissal from office. Bishop Bourget did not approve of her being dismissed from the community;[10] but, in the general confusion the chaplain succeeded in convincing him, at least, to banish her to St. Genevieve.

## The Exile and Disappearance

Indeed, Esther Blondin was exiled.[11] From November 1854, to August 1857, she was not to return, even once, to St. Jacques. Then she was permitted to reappear for the holidays; but even

---

[8] See *Ibid.,* pp. 390-391.

[9] *Ibid.,* Letter from Father Maréchal to Mother Marie Angèle, General Superior, undated, but written after September 13, 1854, pp. 602-603.

[10] Even the bishop's reasons for disallowing her expulsion were overshadowed by the unfavourable opinion he had formed of her. "We must not forget that every community needs some subjects who will be very trying to the rest... Nevertheless, it is better to keep them than to risk worse results," he wrote to Father Maréchal. See Sister Marie Jean de Pathmos, S.S.A., *Dossier sur la vie et les vertus,* p. 261.

[11] On the circumstances surrounding this exile, mention must be made of a letter sent to Bishop Joseph Larocque, administrator of the diocese of Montreal since the departure of Bishop Bourget for Rome on October 23, 1854. In that letter, dated October 25, Father Maréchal tried to show that the sickness of the foundress was a deception and he added to his virulence a medical certificate which he himself had obtained as "proof" of his affirmations. (It is to be noted that the doctor who wrote the certificate was contradicting himself, since he had said she was dying just a few weeks earlier.) Relying on

then, for two consecutive summers, she was whisked away again as soon as possible: "My retreat over, I was allowed only a few days in the community to rest from the fatigue of the trip (...) and I was immediately sent with another sister to keep the mission at St. Ambroise (...) My Lord, to me, the reasons they gave me have as little foundation as the ones they gave me last year, when I came back to my dear community after an absence of three years, such a long and painful absence (...) My Lord, they told me just a short time ago that Father Chaplain had said that if I stayed in the community, he would leave; I did not want to believe it, but their attitude towards me last year and this year tells me it is true, and that in the community I am a very heavy burden to him. My Lord, if Father Chaplain had in view only the glory of God, the salvation of my soul and that of all the sisters, and the general good of the whole community, as he convinced them he had in order to have them approve his conduct and to give them an unfavourable impression of me, as he did, it seems to me that he should not have had anything to fear from my presence in the community. Why does he take such care to send me away as soon as I reappear among my dear daughters, that they cannot suffer me there; it is a sharp sword that pierces me to the depths of my soul, and which reopens all the wounds I have received." [12]

This exile was just one of several forms of persecution, more subtle but not less violent. One of her contemporaries said that after her dismissal, the foundress was cut off from all communication with her community. She was forbidden to write to anyone but the person who replaced her as superior. Those sis-

---

these statements, Bishop Larocque ordered the immediate departure of the foundress from St. Jacques. This happened on just a few hours' notice and in the middle of the night. See, Sister Marie Jean de Pathmos, S.S.A., *Dossier sur la vie et les vertus,* pp. 262 and 305-306.

[12] *The Correspondence of Mother Marie Anne,* Letter to Bishop Bourget, August 18, 1858, pp. 175-177. To justify their conduct, the authorities told the sisters that the foundress had asked to retire to St. Ambroise. It is not hard to imagine the climate of confusion that reigned in the community. See Sister Marie Jean de Pathmos, S.S.A., *Dossier sur la vie et les vertus,* p. 328.

ters who had kept anything that the foundress had written were put under obligation to burn it.[13] Besides being banished, Esther was also virtually under house arrest. A young sister, 23 years of age, was given the responsibility of reporting Esther's conduct to the superior of St. Jacques. The unhappy spy protested directly to the bishop. She told him she could not do it without aggravating the foundress's already deep hurts. She had a director, the young sister said, and it was up to him to lead her. Then she added that unless the bishop ordered her to do so she would not make any reports.[14] So the foundress was really imprisoned for her opinions. She was like a prisoner, isolated from her sisters. Her good name was under attack, and she was not given the right to defend herself.

It could even be said that she disappeared, though of course not physically. In our own day, Pierre Toulat, secretary for the Commission for Justice and Peace, makes a statement about disappearance. He speaks of the degradation of persons given no consideration as persons and no judgment on their actions. He tells of their brutal uprooting from their daily existence, isolated without recourse or help. They are put under arrest without any control of their lives and without any defense. They become part of a process of internment that has no relationships and no limits. The "disappeared" are repudiated, eliminated, reduced, humiliated.[15] This was certainly the psychological circumstance imposed on Esther Blondin when she was sent to St. Genevieve. Three years later, this treatment had lost none of its harshness. The general secretary wrote to tell the foundress in the summer of 1857: "The sisters who are with you call you Mother, or Superior, or Foundress; the others address you correctly. This diversity causes remarks to be made (...) Moreover, it leads the sisters to think that you show little humility in allowing titles you

---

[13] See *Positio,* p. 402.

[14] See *Ibid.,* Letter from Sister Marie Michel to Bishop Bourget, September 1, 1856, p. 402.

[15] See Pierre Toulat, "Le disparu et la dégradation", in *Croissance des jeunes nations,* 233, Novembre 1981, p. 40.

have no right to bear."[16] The idea was to deny her very existence. She had already lost her credibility with many of her sisters who had been won over by Father Maréchal. Nevertheless, some of the sisters remained faithful to her and wanted to elect her superior in 1857.[17] Did this fact alarm the chaplain? Quite possibly it did, because the generalate, which was under his influence,[18] attacked her relentlessly throughout 1858.

## The Definitive Destitution

In January, Esther requested permission to meet her sisters who were leaving for Vancouver Island. She was refused this last contact with them. She expressed the dream she cherished of visiting them some day, after her death. The superior's ill-will drove her to upbraid Esther: "As for your wish to go to see your sisters in Vancouver after your death, if God had deemed you useful for this mission, he would certainly have turned the will of your superiors in your favour. It is His ordinary means, not having recourse to miracles, to satisfy your curiosity. I beg you do not speak in this manner for the sake of your reputation and that of the community."[19]

At the age of 49, hemmed in on every side, the foundress was on the verge of another dismissal. This time the cause was her

---

[16] *The Correspondence of Mother Marie Anne,* Letter from Sister Marie Jeanne de Chantal, undated, but prior to August 10, 1857, p. 124. Yet, in a letter dated November 23, 1857, Sister Marie Michel who was living with Esther, requested from Bishop Bourget, for herself and her companions, the authorization to continue addressing the foundress by the title "Mother". See Sister Marie Jean de Pathmos, S.S.A., *Dossier sur la vie et les vertus,* pp. 363-364. Also, see *The Correspondence of Mother Marie Anne,* p. 123.

[17] See *Positio,* p. 444.

[18] Since 1855, Father Maréchal had taken upon himself to be the secretary for the general superior, and he attended council meetings. He continued this interference with subsequent superiors, as well.

[19] *The Correspondence of Mother Marie Anne,* Letter from Mother Marie de la Purification, General Superior, February 6, 1858, p. 141.

alleged incompetence to run the St. Genevieve convent-school. For the past few years, she had been accused of not sending enough financial help to the motherhouse in St. Jacques. In February 1858, however, the attacks intensified. A letter announced, first of all, that she would be given help. Esther, who was not deceived, replied: "You tell me to be patient, that soon you will send me a helper. I did not ask for help; but, if you judge it expedient for the good of the house to name another directress, send her (...) after all, you will only be carrying out a plan you made a long time ago. But, since I am in this mission (not) by the competent authority of the community, but by the private authority of His Grace the Bishop of Montreal, I am sending him, one of these days, a faithful account of the temporal administration of the mission."[20]

The following March 7, the superior of St. Jacques wrote personally to the pastor of St. Genevieve, asking him to arbitrate the dispute over a government subsidy to the school directed by the foundress. The latter proposed to use the money for which she herself had applied to the Superintendent of Education. She had been particularly concerned for the welfare of the students and the sisters who lived so meagerly. The pastor agreed to be mediator and audited all the books and accounts of the school. Then, after having read all the business letters involved on both sides, he made known his findings to the superior of St. Jacques. Firstly, the mission was not only in debt, but without indemnity; yet, there were no useless expenses, far from it, and it was being administered with care. Secondly, government school subsidies could not be sent to the community unless there was a surplus. The pastor ended his report with the remark that after careful consideration of all the facts, he had come to the conclusion that Sister Marie Anne was being persecuted. He said that persecution was the lot of foundresses in this world; that there seemed to be a need for trials. He concluded by saying that they were blessed, a thousand times blessed, who could bear such trials

[20] *Ibid.,* Letter to Sister Marie Jeanne de Chantal, end of February 1858, pp. 146-147.

with patience.[21] This stand taken by Father Lefaivre had several repercussions. The most surprising one was a letter from the general superior to Bishop Bourget. In it she insinuated that Father Lefaivre had meddled in community affairs at the instigation of the foundress. The bishop probably never suspected that he was being deceived. He certainly did not know about the letter from the general superior to Father Lefaivre. The bishop settled the issue. He wrote to her on April 19, 1858, "I think there is nothing else you can do but to recall Sister Marie Anne to St. Jacques as soon as possible where you will show her all the kindness you can by giving her every opportunity to rest without harming anyone."[22]

Esther Blondin had no idea that she had fallen from the bishop's grace, and she expressed the wish to meet with him. Contrary to the right that the sisters had by the constitutions, she was apparently refused the authorization to do so. She wrote to him: "Allow me to ask Your Grace whether it is no longer permitted to the religious of our community to see the first ecclesiastical superior when in need of meeting him? Twice now I have asked Reverend Mother to go to the city (...) but I was told that she knows what to think on that point, that I could write to Your Grace. My Lord, I know without any doubt, that they fear my interviews with you (...) they wrote to me a while ago that all permissions for trips the sisters from the missions have to make were to be referred to the superior, and to her alone, which is quite contrary to the constitutions Your Grace wrote."[23] But Bishop Bourget did nothing about her complaints.[24] When July

---

[21] See *Positio,* Letter from Father Louis Marie Lefaivre to Mother Marie de la Purification, General Superior, March 29, 1858, p. 414.

[22] *Dossier sur la vie et les vertus,* Letter from Bishop Bourget to Mother Marie de la Purification, General Superior, April 19, 1858, pp. 396-397.

[23] *Ibid.,* Letter to Bishop Bourget, June 21, 1858, pp. 157-158.

[24] Bishop Bourget's esteem towards Esther Blondin diminished noticeably and gradually as Father Maréchal's denigrations continued. Some historical documents show that the bishop of Montreal was particularly kind towards the priest and gave the mandates that Maréchal requested for himself and his brother Napoléon, to whom he apologized for having caused him the greatest

came, the foundress, as she had foreseen, was recalled from St. Genevieve.

After her retreat, she was to be sent off to St. Ambroise de Kildare for the holidays. But before she left, another act of violence was perpetrated against her, this time in her most fundamental human rights. The superior, Mother Marie de la Purification, took from the foundress, without her knowledge, certain incriminating letters. The superior no doubt intended to destroy these. Here is how Esther Blondin made the matter known to the bishop: "My Lord, they used a kind of violence against me after the retreat. I said nothing, I offered no resistance, I gave up everything, but I waited for the opportunity to tell Your Grace something about it. After the retreat Mother Superior told all the sisters to whom she had written to return all the letters they had not burned; as for me, I had quite a few. I gave her all those I had and I was very glad to have her see them all at once. It is not of these that I wish to speak; it is of those that Your Grace gave me the honour of writing to me since the foundation of the community; not those which had to stay in the archives, but those which were personal to me, and two from Father Chaplain, which I thought I should remit to Your Grace, and many others besides. I do not think that any superior has the right to demand that these letters be given to her, since she must not read letters which she knows come from Your Grace (...) I think I put them in my travelling bag, and I found only the envelope; I spoke to her about it; she looked surprised. What leads me to believe that it was she who took them is that I told her I thought I had them with me and that I would see which ones I could give her. She asked where they were if I had them with me; I told her (because) I could see that I would gain nothing by hiding it. My Lord, I have many more things to tell Your Grace, but I am already too long."[25] Judging by his total silence, the bishop was unmoved

distress in suggesting that he go to St. Henri Parish in 1867. As a matter of fact, after that event, Bishop Bourget never again asked the pastor of St. Jacques to move from that parish. See Sister Marie Jean de Pathmos, S.S.A., *Dossier sur la vie et les vertus,* pp. 262 note 31, 488, 490 note 5, 492-498 and 528.

[25] *The Correspondence of Mother Marie Anne,* Letter to Bishop Bourget, August 18, 1858, pp. 177-178.

by such an abuse of power and by that act of injustice.[26] But this was not all. In the summer of 1858, the name of the foundress did not even appear on the list of nominations. Nor was it listed among the personnel of the community; she was sentenced to a year of rest. The one who, according to her own expression, "remained zero all year" would henceforth be in St. Jacques in the shadow of Father Maréchal and the sisters he had won over to his cause.[27]

## The Endless Fallout

By fateful coincidence, Esther Blondin was named five years later to Lachine, where she was to find another Father Maréchal, Napoléon, brother of the first and of the same stamp. He greeted her with the remark, "It is through charity, Sister, that you have been made to come here." To which the foundress replied, "It is not just starting from today that the charity of God has gone before me, and how I am at rest in it!"[28] Esther would not be really free of the presence of the brothers Maréchal until 1872. It was the year of the elections of the general officers.[29] A contemporary of the foundress says that after all

---

[26] Bishop Bourget wrote his last letter to Esther Blondin in response to one she wrote him to share her joy at being allowed to work after a year of enforced rest. The bishop was kind to her, but his letter marked the end of their relationship.

[27] The community was marked by the chaplain's influence. This can be explained in part by the tacit support of Bishop Bourget; and the youth of the superiors who succeeded the foundress.

[28] Sister Marie Jean de Pathmos, S.S.A., *Dossier sur la vie et les vertus,* p. 413. See also pp. 490-492 on the Maréchal brothers.

[29] This freedom went back legally to 1869. That was the year the pastor of Lachine, Father Nazaire Piché, became ecclesiastical superior of the community. He was replacing Father Napoléon Maréchal who was asked to resign after an involvement in spiritism. Father Louis Adolphe had ceded his powers to his younger brother two years previously. Nevertheless, in 1872, both brothers still meddled in the community. They were trying to organize the elections of the general superior and her councillors, as they had always done. Father

ties with the Maréchals had been severed by the community, the first free chapter (free, that is, from psychological pressures) elected Mother Marie Anne to the general council. This was eighteen years after her dismissal in 1854. "Her daughters had remained sincerely attached to her."[30] There is a good deal of truth in this testimony. In 1878, she was again elected to the general council. Nevertheless, in spite of these two elections the foundress was kept on the outside. She carried a title with no real responsibility, and it often happened that the secretary of the council signed official reports in her place. A sister reported: "The foundress's advice was never sought. She had no part in decision-making. She learned community news when the whole community did. Whenever she saw the Mother General whispering to one of the councillors, she would ask someone, 'There is no bad news for the community, is there?' And let us not forget that Mother Marie Anne was herself a councillor at the time."[31] The prejudice that had given her the reputation of incompetence had held on for a long time.

A destiny as tragic as hers, woven of repression and betrayal, had been orchestrated by some and tolerated by others, regardless of the intentions of the persons involved. Esther Blondin suffered the harshest violence through insidious propaganda, and she was like a prisoner because of her opinion. In the very heart of her community, they tried by every means to deny her prophetic mission of foundress[32] and to erase the least traces of it. It was not until thirteen years after her death that Vaudreuil was officially recognized as the birthplace of her community.

---

Piché was aware of their unfair manoeuverings (depriving certain sisters of their right to vote, double-voting for others...) He reported this to Bishop Bourget, who decided to preside over the elections himself. The Maréchal brothers had managed to hold on to the community as a trusteeship for a long time. Sister Marie Jean de Pathmos, S.S.A., *Dossier sur la vie et les vertus,* pp. 415-416, 454-456 and 479.

[30] *Positio,* p. 445.

[31] *Ibid.,* p. 450.

[32] One fact, among many, testifies to this. In a letter, dated January 26, 1867, the general superior, Mother Marie Jeanne de Chantal designated the

# The Violent Destiny of the Prophets

## MOHANDAS GANDHI

Mohandas Gandhi was partly contemporary to these events, and he shared the tragic lot of the prophets. Fifteen years after his decision to devote his life to active nonviolence, he had his first encounter with violence. He was still living in South Africa when he refused, one day, to obey a civil law he considered unjust. The colonial government of Transvaal required that all, and only, Indian citizens be fingerprinted. They also had to carry a registration card on their person at all times. Gandhi warned those who had already started to follow him: "We may have to go to jail, where we may be insulted. We may have to go hungry and suffer extreme heat or cold. Hard labour may be imposed upon us. We may be flogged by rude warders. We may be fined heavily and our property may be attached and held up to auction (...) We may be deported (...) some of us may fall ill and die. In short, therefore, it is not at all impossible that we may have to endure every hardship that we can imagine, and wisdom lies in pledging ourselves on the understanding that we shall have to suffer all that and worse." [33] He was right.

Soon after, he served his first jail term, the first of a long series. During the course of his battle, he learned after a while that he could negotiate with the government of Transvaal. He could make some concessions. Some of his own people then accused him of treason. He received death threats from the extremists among his partisans. He was savagely beaten by one of them, Mir Alam, on February 10, 1908. [34] At age 38 the *Mahatma* reaped the violence that his mission aroused. He soon

---

two Maréchal brothers as "founders of the community". This shows the hold these two priests had on the authorities of that time. It also shows to what point their conduct encouraged this interpretation of the facts. See Sister Marie Jean de Pathmos, S.S.A., *Dossier sur la vie et les vertus,* pp. 522-527.

[33] Robert Payne, *The Life and Death of Mahatma Gandhi,* pp. 163-164.

[34] See *Ibid.,* p. 181.

served a second term, and this time it took many forms of hard labour: "For nine hours a day, he was forced to break stones, dig pits, and work with road gangs. He was sent out to work in the market square at Volksrust, and the European warder kept urging him to work harder, shouting: 'Come on, Gandhi! Come on Gandhi!' Sometimes an Indian prisoner would faint with exhaustion in the heat. Gandhi would return to the prison at the end of a day's work with stiff limbs and swollen wrists."[35]

When Gandhi settled in India, the same scenario of repression was enacted. In 1922, soon after his first massive civil disobedience campaign, he was sentenced to six years in prison. In 1930, he was jailed again without trial, a month after the Salt March which had been a challenge to the colonial government. This time, it was with some of the leaders of Congress who were also implicated. In 1932, in Bombay, he was arrested for violation of the government's emergency laws. Again there was no trial, the viceroy simply ordered his arrest! Gandhi spent much of his life in prison, at one point it was seven years divided into short terms. He finally gave as his home address Yeravda Prison.

The negotiations he pursued with British authorities sometimes took him to London. During one of these conferences, Churchill insulted him one day, by describing his appearance "alarming and also nauseating and humiliating spectacle of this one-time inner temple lawyer, now seditious fakir, striding half-naked up the steps of the viceroy's palace, there to negotiate and parley on equal terms."[36]

One of Gandhi's greatest nightmares was the violence which infiltrated the noncooperation campaign he directed. It sometimes happened, also, that when Gandhi was imprisoned, riots broke out in reprisal. Such reactions haunted him and he was always looking for ways to prevent and to eliminate them. To a certain extent, his mission at the end was bathed in shadow and in blood. As India neared independence, the rival Hindu and Moslem groups fought to the death and the country was ravaged

---

[35] *Ibid.*, p. 191.

[36] Gerald Gold, *Gandhi a Pictorial Biography,* p. 91.

by civil war: "All his life Gandhi had dreamed of an India at peace, bringing peace to the world by her example (...) Now, at the very moment when freedom was being wrested from the British, the dream of peaceful India was shattered. The savagery of the murders in East Bengal was on a vast, unprecedented scale."[37] In November 1946, Gandhi travelled through that devastated region calling his countrymen to forgiveness and unity. This was a period of self-question on these massacres, the causes of which escaped him.

Being troubled, he often spoke of his own death, which he sensed was near; and he lived with misgivings about his mission. He was not really recognized as mediator between rival Indian factions, and like Esther Blondin at certain times, was keenly aware of being powerless. At times, he was the target of the hatred that tore his country; a Moslem spat in his face, crowds called as he passed by, "Death to Gandhi." Some challenged him, "If you are a *Mahatma,* perform a miracle and save India."[38] On January 20, 1948, someone threw a bomb near him, a sign of protest against his policy of Hindu-Moslem friendship. Ten days later, a Hindu fanatic assassinated him. Mission accomplished? Without doubt, but under circumstances that seem so very contradictory.


## MARTIN LUTHER KING

The same mystery marked the life of Martin Luther King. In 1956, at the very beginning of his public prophetic undertaking, he faced violence. His wife, Coretta, affirmed that during the boycotting of buses in Montgomery, their telephone rang day and night with threats, insults, or streams of obscenities.[39] These threats were already something other than malicious jokes, or simple tactics aimed at terrorizing. Twice, a bomb was thrown

---

[37] Robert Payne, *The Life and Death of Mahatma Gandhi,* p. 519.

[38] *Ibid.,* p. 550.

[39] See Coretta Scott King, *My Life with Martin Luther King Jr.,* p. 11.

on the gallery of their house, and the family barely escaped the catastrophe. Martin Luther King, therefore, faced the possibility of violent death for himself and his family, very early in his mission. In September 1957, he came within a hair's breadth of death when, in public, a woman stabbed him. On another occasion, during a public demonstration in Chicago, he was knocked to the ground. Someone had aimed a rock at his head, though he was not seriously injured.

Martin Luther King experienced violence also during the course of some of his arrests. A biographer records that on Wednesday, September 3, 1958, a police officer who disliked him stopped him on the street: "At the jail, King was searched and then 'pushed and kicked' into a cell. He was booked on a charge of loitering and released on bond (...) When he reached his home that day, he told the assembled friends and aides, 'I've had enough of this thing.' After a day of prayerful considerations and a long talk with Coretta, he decided to go to jail instead of paying the fine."[40] This event marked the turning point in his life. From that day, he used the violence against him as a weapon of peace in the service of his mission.

His arrests and his numerous jail terms became facts which awakened consciences and jostled racial prejudice. At times, the consciences of the security agents themselves were stirred; such as, Chief Laurie Pritchett: "He would allow the protesters to demonstrate up to a point, then he would say, 'Now we're going to break this up. If you don't disperse, you'll be arrested.' Our people were given fair warning. Often they would refuse to disperse, and would drop on their knees and pray. Chief Pritchett would bow his head with them while they prayed; then, of course, he would arrest them and the people would to go jail singing."[41] Such experiences revealed the quiet earnestness of those who followed Martin Luther King.

Around 1960, the prophet felt another totally unexpected shock: he was unjustly accused of fraud in declaring his revenue

---

[40] Lerone Bennett, *What Manner of Man,* p. 97.

[41] Coretta Scott King, *My Life with Martin Luther King, Jr.,* p. 204.

for the years 1956 and 1958. Despite a trial that cleared him, the notoriety caused by the false accusation affected King more than anything else. He began to suffer from guilt feelings, even though he was innately honest. When he managed to pull himself together, he understood that the strategy was aimed at undermining his prestige. It was also meant to thwart the movement of which he was the leader. "The indictments," he said, "were another attempt by the state of Alabama to harass me because of the position I've taken in the civil rights struggle."[42]

Other sufferings also wove the prophetic destiny of Minister King. He found the tension of being a public figure particularly trying. Beyond the exigencies of his mission, he wanted to spend more time with his wife and four children. He also felt bad that he was neglecting his Baptist Congregation. His private life became less and less his own as his involvement took on wider scope.

These deprivations did not spare him from bitter criticism. In 1963, during the Birmingham campaign, Martin Luther King received a collective letter from the most eminent religious persons of that city who "denounced him as an 'interloper' and 'extremist' who made 'unwise and untimely' demonstrations."[43] That kind of treatment put him in the same boat as Esther Blondin, even though they lived in different eras and in such different circumstances. Among the blacks, some came down on him: those who were already recognized as powerful in the system; activists and intellectuals from the North who opted for violent solutions, and the nationalists who saw him as the unwitting tool of the whites. He was angrily called "Uncle Tom," and they turned away in aversion from the only weapon he used, nonviolent protest.

Martin Luther King understood the frustration that underlay this anger, but he sometimes became dizzy before the tide of violence which he could no longer stem. The revolt of the Harlem ghetto in the summer of 1964 affected him particularly, and

---

[42] Lerone Bennett, *What Manner of Man,* p. 115.

[43] See *Ibid.,* p. 140.

when he received the Nobel Peace Prize, the following December, he bore that drama in his heart.

Many of his collaborators gave up at some time or other, and some did not understand his speeches for world peace. They could not or would not follow him outside the limits of their own immediate cause. The pastor also met an increasing number of people who became indifferent as the years went by. In Cleveland, in November 1967, he admitted that it had been hard, very hard, that he had never seen such apathetic people. He said he could not interest them in anything.[44] Shamed, fawned upon, derided, applauded, compassed about, hounded, or slandered, Martin Luther King pursued his mission to the end. He was assassinated in Memphis on April 4, 1968. He was 39 years old.

## HÉLDER CÂMARA

The destiny of Dom Hélder Câmara was no less tragic. Furthermore, his fate turned out to be remarkably like Esther Blondin's own. He brought on himself, through his commitment and his outspokenness, insidious and acute suffering. As he said, he did not have the advantage of a frank, open, and straightforward clash with his opponents: "When Gandhi went on a hunger strike, the whole world was grieved and there was no empire, however powerful, capable of resisting the moral pressure which arose from the four corners of the Earth. But let us suppose that the established regime had left Gandhi without a voice, had placed his closest and dearest collaborators in prison, that it had spread about them the worst slanders (...) what would the apostle of nonviolence have been able to do?"[45] That was the sort of violence that the Bishop of Recife endured for many years.

The defamatory campaign against him after Vatican II, led him to a form of poverty he had hitherto not imagined. "When

---

[44] See John J. Ansbro, *Martin Luther King, Jr.: The Making of a Mind*, pp. 225-227.

[45] Hélder Câmara, *Spiral of Violence*, pp. 48-49.

I lost my own freedom of speech, my reputation, my very name, (...) I understood that poverty is something altogether different from a wooden pectoral cross or a very simple residence."[46] This action, the first significant one of his life was summed up in his nickname "the red Bishop." This showed the atmosphere of suspicion, slander and scorn that encompassed him. Dom Hélder Câmara wrote about this kind of shock treatment: "Experience has taught us that the treatment accorded those who act in the field of social work varies completely according to whether one stops at social welfare or feels the necessity to go beyond it and struggle for the human advancement of men who are not yet men. If you stop with social welfare (...) you'll be accorded consideration and esteem. But the day you realize that all this is not enough and that it is necessary to fight for the right of your brothers dragged down by misery to live as human beings, you will fall under suspicion and be looked on as a subversive, a pawn of the communists. We have even witnessed the absurdity of seeing one of the most beautiful expressions of the democratic vocabulary, *conscientização,* condemned as a word that, if not actually red, was certainly tinged with pink."[47] The bishop bore the most stinging calumnies, unable even to defend himself because the Brazilian government forbade him public speech.

This "civil death" and disappearance constitute the most striking resemblances linking him to Esther Blondin: "For ten years, (...) Brazilian newspaper, radio, and television were prohibited from publishing or broadcasting any news whatever about me, positive or negative, or any document from me or about me. I no longer received any invitations except those of a strictly religious nature, since it was known that the government would not be pleased."[48] As he himself said, after having enjoyed great fame and general esteem, he was reduced to nothing. He was "reduced to nothing, less than nothing... fallen into silence, like

---

[46] Id., *Questions for Living,* p. 35.
[47] Id., *Revolution through Peace,* pp. 132-133.
[48] Id., *Questions for Living,* p. 2.

a tomb,"[49] thus overtaking Esther Blondin and so many other prophets.

Besides enduring his own share of false reports, disgrace and repression, Dom Hélder Câmara also suffered from these indignities imposed on his co-workers. This anguish united him especially closely to his confrère Oscar Romero. He explained: "It is clear that anyone who, in proclaiming the Gospel, demands justice as a condition of peace, risks imprisonment (...) More serious still for the priest than being put in prison is not being put in prison, but seeing in prison all around him militant laymen who have simply echoed the evangelical message."[50] Sometimes this agony reached a climax: "I believe I would infinitely have preferred to be tortured myself than to have my collaborators tortured (...) assassinated. It's absolutely horrible. The number of times I have had to go to hospitals or prisons, or even to a morgue, to collect or identify collaborators who had disappeared, priests and laymen."[51]

He went through many persecutions and threats, and he was isolated by his brother-bishops. In spite of all this, he still had the courage to affirm in his old age, "To despair of the Church would be to despair of Christ! But to live in the Church means always wishing it to be more faithful to the Gospel. This is something that will have to be suffered for and striven for in each new generation."[52]

## OSCAR ROMERO

Oscar Romero experienced a similar fate, especially during the last years of his life. "If I gave the impression before of being more 'discreet' and 'spiritual;' it was because I sincerely believed that thus I responded to the Gospel."[53] But from the

[49] Id., *The Conversions of a Bishop*, p. 110.

[50] Id., *Spiral of Violence*, pp. 49-50.

[51] Id., *The Conversions of a Bishop*, p. 200.

[52] Id., *Questions for Living*, p. 37.

[53] James R. Brockman, *The Word Remains*, p. 115.

moment that he became archbishop of San Salvador, he discovered new dimensions of his pastoral ministry and he resolutely embraced them. The difficulties were not far behind, and in first place were the attacks on him in the press. One of these appeared in the *Prensa Grafica* of May 24, 1977, signed by the Committee for the Betterment of the Catholic Church. Among other things it said: "A few bad priests are causing most serious harm to the Catholic Church and the whole country. And it is not understood or granted that the archbishop carries his affection (...) to the point of not wanting to see the faults of these bad priests. Rather he blames those who censure them, who denounce their misdeeds, who desire a purification of the clergy."[54] In a general way, the suggestions of the presss are more virulent, and with offensive cartoons to match. Pineda Quinteros, a priest of the diocese, added fuel to the fire. This recalcitrant priest, having taken over by force the church and rectory of Quezaltepeque, had also publicly burned the decree of suspension that Bishop Romero had sent him and the priest excommunicated his bishop! Thus, he was a ready-made collaborator for press and government.

More painful still than the false denunciations was the division in the Salvadorian episcopacy. This kind of division Esther Blondin experienced at the heart of her own community. Bishop Romero, for example, took the occasion of a stay in Rome during the 1977 synod, to criticize Salvadorian pastoral ministry... Now Romero was delegated to the synod by his confrères. There were other outward signs of division: the negative reports that flowed into Rome denigrating the Archbishop of San Salvador. In fact, his journal entry for May 18, 1979, mentioned a document that Bishops Aparicio, Alvarez, Barrera and Revelo had just sent to Rome. The title of the document was "Politico-Religious Situation of El Salvador." It was, according to a biographer: "simply an attack on Romero, portraying the archbishop as at once naive and wily, imposing a politicized Marxist idea of pastoral practice on the Church of the country, interfering in other dioceses,

---

[54] *Ibid.*, p. 57.

led by a group of radical priests, associated with the 'Marxist' FECCAS-UTC and BPR, blessing terrorism, and defaming the government."[55] Such ruptures at the heart of the episcopacy constituted for the prophet "the division that Christ had announced even among members of the same family."[56] He lived a similar situation with the papal Nuncio.

Abroad, he was supported and honoured as the defender of the rights of man. The University of Georgetown in Washington, and later the University of Louvain, granted him titles of honour. In his own country, however, the vise was tightening on him.

During the summer before his death, he was made to get out of his car while authorities searched him. His homilies were taped and he was kept under surveillance. Threats became more direct. On February 24, 1980, he said, "This week I received notice that I am on the list of those who are to be eliminated next week."[57] "He felt terror at it (...) But he did not for that leave his post and his duty."[58] On the following March 10, a workman discovered 72 sticks of dynamite in the cathedral. Oscar Romero went to his destiny without flinching. He demanded inquiries into the disappearance of people, and denounced unjustified arrests. On March 24, 1980, he suffered the ultimate violence. He was assassinated among his own while he celebrated the Eucharist.

The following day, the Salvadorean Conference of Bishops published a communqué. This time it was unanimous: "From the time he became archbishop, Romero tirelessly proclaimed the message of salvation and denounced with inexorable vigor institutionalized injustice and abuses against human rights and the inalienable dignity of the human being made to the image of God. This gained him the esteem of friends and strangers, but it also aroused the animosity of those who felt uncomfortable from the

[55] *Ibid.,* p. 162.
[56] *Ibid.,* p. 116.
[57] *Ibid.,* p. 210.
[58] *Ibid.,* p. 211.

force of his evangelical word and his witness. For being faithful to the word, he fell like the great prophets."[59]

So the tragic destiny of the prophets is inseparable from their mission. They face all the violence they arouse from the mere fact of their commitment and their outspokenness. They experience the final consequence of their mission, according to the paradox of the Gospel itself. Rejected, they bring together; ill treated, they forgive; killed, they open the doors to hope...

---

[59] *Ibid.,* p. 221.

# Chapter 4

# A Prophetic Risk

*They used a kind of violence towards me...*
*I offered no resistance...*

Esther Blondin

*In its positive form, nonviolence means the*
*largest love, the greatest charity.*

Gandhi

Prophets are involved on the spot in the service of the most marginalized human beings. Their word is uncompromising, and their tragic destiny is a consequence of the choices they make. Over and above their involvement, their word and their destiny, they all share an astonishing freedom of heart. This comes from being disarming, nonviolent and forgiving. Living this way is a risk, given the struggle they engage in with such passion and wholeheartedness. Consciously, deliberately, from their innermost selves, they choose to love where oppression, hate, even death overshadow them. It is their relationship with God that seems to be the foundation and source of the risks they take. This, at least, is what stands out from their profoundly faith-filled lives and the prayer experience which is their thread.

## The Option for Nonviolence

This was a striking reality in the life of Esther Blondin. From the moment of Father Maréchal's arrival in St. Jacques, she tried to ease the tensions caused by his meddling. She wrote the following to her bishop and then, on several occasions, repeated the same kind of request, "My Lord, allow me to ask you in all simplicity whether it is the Reverend Father Paré who is our superior, or whether it is Father Chaplain, and what are the duties we owe to these two gentlemen?"[1] Esther constantly searched for ways of mutual understanding and peace without sacrificing either truth or justice. She acted with the same freedom after her dismissal. She did not complain to her bishop, but she was con-

---

[1] *The Correspondence of Mother Marie Anne,* Letter to Bishop Bourget, October 4, 1853, p. 72.

cerned for the good of her sisters: "At last I am relieved of the heavy burden of being a superior (...) I carried out faithfully what Your Grace ordered me to do (...) For me, my Lord, what hurts me at the moment, is not to have done all the good I would have wished to have done for the glory of God and the good of the community."[2] Following this drama, Esther looked to God for the strength to pursue her way without bitterness or violence. Several times during the illness following her dismissal she even sought forgiveness from Father Maréchal, hoping for a complete reconciliation. One of her contemporaries said that on the way to her exile, St. Genevieve, she searched the roadside for mission crosses. They were scattered here and there, along the way, and at each one she prayed. "My good Saviour, please take away whatever is inordinate in me, so that I may go wherever you want me to be."[3] Doubtless it was in the "risked" experience of this unique relationship that she found the inspiration and courage she needed. Unilateral disarmament in the face of her antagonists was a risk.

She continued to show the same attitude of nonviolence through the following years in her contacts with authorities. When she deemed it better to remain silent, even her silence was free of all pressure and spirit of vengeance. In a letter to her superior in August 1857, she made a simple comment. "As to the letter from Sister Marie Jeanne de Chantal, I do not believe I need to answer it."[4] Six months later, she wrote directly to the secretary of the generalate: "I will not undertake to answer what you express in your letter. I will be satisfied to tell you that I am neither displeased with nor against you, nor against anybody. Neither am I reproaching anybody... God will know in His wisdom how to discern the false from the true, and to reward each one according to his deeds. In the meantime, let us be at peace

---

[2] *Ibid.,* Letter to Bishop Bourget, August 20, 1854, pp. 99-100.

[3] *Positio,* p. 395.

[4] *The Correspondence of Mother Marie Anne,* Letter to Mother Marie de la Purification, General Superior, August 10, 1857, p. 125.

and united by the bond of the pure charity of Jesus Christ."[5] The risk of making such a gratuitous relationship found its source in God. From this wellspring, Esther Blondin seemed to draw an inexhaustible reserve of nonviolence towards those who deceived, humiliated or maligned her. Father Lefaivre of St. Genevieve gave this beautiful testimony of her in a letter he had sent to the general superior of that time. "I have never heard her speak anything but good of you and of all your sisters. She told me herself many times that she is very pleased to see you as superior, and always spoke to me of you with respect."[6]

A few years later, as the foundress arrived at the new mother-house in Lachine, the Chaplain Napoléon Maréchal let her know that she was being received through charity. "Yes, Father," she replied, "God's charity has always anticipated my need and how well I rest in it."[7] Esther Blondin pursued her mission through an active and benevolent nonviolence by which she healed the deep ruptures of her community and continued to mother it in the background.

## The Weapons of Peace

Being "disarming" also marked her relationships with her sisters. On August 15, 1873, the community was celebrating the twenty-fourth anniversary of the first investiture. An address was read "to the foundresses." A witness related that on this occasion: "Sister Marie Anne replied with a dignity and affection which brought tears to the eyes of some of the sisters. She recalled the first days of the community and she assured us that the greater part of the wishes she addressed to heaven every day were for us and for the good of our little community."[8] That

---

[5] *Ibid.,* Letter to Sister Marie Jeanne de Chantal, February 1858, pp. 138-139.

[6] *Positio,* Letter from Father Louis Marie Lefaivre to Mother Marie de la Purification, General Superior, April 14, 1858, p. 537.

[7] *Ibid.,* pp. 433-434.

[8] *Ibid.,* p. 424.

was the foundress. She had no concern for her own rights. She always put her own heart at risk, her heart that overflowed in her letters to her sisters far away: "If I cannot write to each one separately, tell them all that I remember them faithfully, that I feel obliged more than anyone else to pray every day for them, for their happiness and that of the flock confided to their care, as well as for their own sanctification."[9] No, the foundress had not laid down her weapons. She was severely restricted in her action and in her speech, so she deployed what Gandhi called "the finest quality of the heart;"[10] that is, active and affective nonviolence.

Her weapons of predilection were prayer, abundant and heartfelt prayer of intercession, and frequent fasting unless otherwise forbidden. Thus, in September 1855, the deposed foundress made a decision to fast daily, until the end of her life. This was to "expiate all the sins which were committed in the community by all the members which then composed it."[11] She kept up this purification fast for two consecutive years, and interrupted it only at the end of October 1857 on the order of her superior. Twenty years later, the chronicles of the motherhouse recorded that Esther Blondin had resumed the practice.[12] These fasts were in addition to regular Catholic fast days during Advent, Lent and on the eve of great liturgical feasts. Despite the rigorism that prevailed in her day, these fasts were nonviolent gestures expressing her struggle for justice and unity.

## The Audacious Pardon

Esther went further than voluntary disarmament, option for nonviolence, and lack of rancour. She forgave. Christian Duquoc

---

[9] *The Correspondence of Mother Marie Anne,* Letter to Sister Marie Joachim, July 2, 1876, p. 204.

[10] Mahatma Gandhi, *The Collected Works of Mahatma Gandhi, XLVI,* p. 2.

[11] *The Correspondence of Mother Marie Anne,* Spiritual Notes, p. 228.

[12] See *Positio,* p. 84.

says that forgiveness is a risk... it exists where someone has the power to threaten another's existence, whether materially or psychologically, where someone violates someone else's rights. So it is not oversight, nor indifference, nor naiveté.[13] On this path, Esther Blondin gave full measure. On September 10, 1854, she was still sick in bed in the infirmary after the shock of her first dismissal from office. She spoke to the chaplain as he brought her Communion. They were pathetic words and they caused a scandal; but in reality, they were a last attempt at reconciliation: "Stop, Minister of Jesus Christ. In the name of God of all charity whom you carry, stop. I know that you have something against me in your heart. If I have afflicted you, forgive me. I have already forgiven you all the harm you have done in the community, all the persecutions you have caused me."[14] These words gave rise to new denunciations, because Father Maréchal cast doubt on the sincerity of the foundress.[15] Furthermore, he demanded public reparation. Mother Marie Angèle, the new superior, wrote of the incident on the same day. "As for me, she has always given me good advice about our Father (Chaplain) and counselled me to show the respect and trust we should have for him and to follow his advice."[16] No matter! The foundress had to expiate the so-called scandal, as witnessed the same superior who said: "She did what Father Superior (Romuald Paré) counselled her to do, by asking pardon of the sisters for the bad example she had given them with regard to Father Director (Maréchal). She is willing to live with him as though she had never had any difficulty with him..."[17] Esther Blon-

---

[13] See Christian Duquoc, *Jésus homme libre,* p. 106.

[14] *Positio,* p. 389.

[15] It is painful to note the skepticism and the insensitivity of Father Maréchal in the face of the pardon which Esther Blondin asked of him and that she offered him several times during the sickness which followed her dismissal. See Sister Marie Jean de Pathmos, S.S.A., *Dossier sur la vie et les vertus,* p. 233.

[16] *Positio,* Letter from Mother Marie Angèle, General Superior, to Bishop Bourget, September 10, 1854, p. 386.

[17] *Ibid.,* p. 386.

din's nonviolence stood out against a backdrop of repression and destruction.[18]

Scarcely two years later, the foundress, exiled in St. Genevieve, extended her forgiveness so far as to wish to invite Father Maréchal to preach the pupils' annual retreat. Nevertheless, she was aware of her personal limitations and she frankly made known her wish to the Bishop of Montreal: "My Lord, I will tell you very simply what happened with regard to the retreat for our pupils. Being one day in the presence of the Blessed Sacrament, (...) the thought of asking the Father Chaplain of the community (...) came to my mind, which was immediately enlightened, and my soul was filled with consolation. (...) I then decided to speak about it to my director who told me that this was a good thought, but that I had to speak to Your Grace about it, and I am doing it with all possible sincerity. My Lord, I have fears which I think are not groundless. If Father Chaplain comes to preach the retreat to our pupils, our two young sisters will naturally want to go to him for confession and for their direction, but for me it is not possible. I fear that it may do more harm than good."[19] The Bishop of Montreal dispelled the fears of the foundress, and she cordially welcomed the chaplain. Such greatness of soul, such forgiveness found plenty of room for exercise during the four years she lived in St. Genevieve. Those were years when the censures and the worries orchestrated by Father Maréchal were preparing her final dismissal and her "zero year."

In the first appointment after that black year, her new function was as sacristan in St. Jacques. Here she was in closer contact with the chaplain, who had become parish priest as well on October 9, 1859. She hoped to succeed in dispelling the unfavourable impression he had of her. She also confided to her bishop: "I will willingly set about it right away, and I have

---

[18] Nowhere in any historical document can there be found from Father Maréchal a single word of regret or admission of his limitations or of his possible wrongdoings in his attitude to Esther Blondin.

[19] *The Correspondence of Mother Marie Anne,* Letter to Bishop Bourget, November 2, 1856, pp. 113-114.

reason to hope that God accepted the little sacrifice I had to make in receiving this office; and as a reward He granted me the grace to change Father Superior's disposition towards me, at least exteriorly. I can only congratulate him for his goodness to me and all his civility towards me, and to bless the Lord for having thus changed his heart." [20] Yes, Esther Blondin took the risk of forgiving. In December of that same year, she reported to her bishop new signs of reconciliation which she had discovered with joy: "The Lord in his infinite goodness continues his work and perfects it more and more. There was still something which was not in accordance with perfect charity. When I had the occasion (...) to meet (Father Maréchal) with a few of my sisters, he still showed himself cold, answered me curtly when I spoke to him, and I noticed little smiles of approval on the faces of those present; I do not need to tell you what I experienced interiorly; the thing speaks for itself. May God be praised! Now all these hardships have disappeared (...) I bless the Lord for it a thousand times." [21]

It is good to recall here that one look at truth, be it ever so free, never saved the truth, or constituted the whole economy of truth. The foundress in Lachine did not deny facts, but she had the reputation of admonishing at once sisters who condemned or passed judgment on those who made her suffer. The chaplain had won over to his cause the most influential sisters in the community. The foundress redoubled her acts of kindness towards them. So we see her, one day during a time of sickness, taking a meal she had prepared into the room of one of these sisters. [22] With regard to that same person another witness affirmed, "Mother Marie Anne came to me several times to ask me discreetly to prepare a good meal for her because she was sick and had no appetite." [23] Until the end Esther Blondin took the risk of showing affective nonviolence.

---

[20] *Ibid.,* Letter to Bishop Bourget, October 17, 1859, p. 185.
[21] *Ibid.,* Letter to Bishop Bourget, December 12, 1859, p. 187.
[22] See *Positio,* p. 552.
[23] *Ibid.,* p. 552.

Her last words were still conciliatory. "For the edification of the sisters," she asked the sister who was sitting up with her, "please, if you have no objection, will you send for Father Maréchal."[24] Even on her deathbed, Esther Blondin saw forgiveness as a "risk action." It was based on the hope that goodness allows the wrongdoer a space other than his logic about wrongdoing. His choice could then be more humane. Again, even on her deathbed, she kept that wonderful freedom of heart. Christian Duquoc says that the one who forgives does not allow himself to be dominated by the hidden evil of the adversary. He does not repair calumny with calumny, defamation with defamation, murder with murder, deceit with deceit. He creates another relationship. This is a call for evil not to be given the last word.[25]

# The Risked Disarmament of the Prophets

## MOHANDAS GANDHI

Mohandas Gandhi's choices were similar to Esther Blondin's. This zealous partisan for India's political independence affirmed what she might have said had his situation been adapted to hers. "I will not purchase my country's freedom at the cost of nonviolence."[26] The disarmament that the *Mahatma* preached, constituted, nevertheless, a veritable weapon. Thus he responded to the terrible massacre at Amritsar, on April 13, 1919. It was a massacre in which soldiers fired for ten minutes on a pacifist crowd trapped in a walled-in space. Gandhi called for a massive boycott. Included were British products, state schools, and the

---

[24] *Ibid.,* p. 600. When Father Maréchal arrived, the patient could no longer speak. The former chaplain gave her a final absolution and assisted at her death. Before leaving her room, he exhorted the sisters who were present to emulate the spirit of prayer of the one who had just left them. See Sister Marie Jean de Pathmos, S.S.A., *Dossier sur la vie et les vertus,* p. 609.

[25] See Christian Duquoc, *Jésus homme libre,* p. 106.

[26] Louis Fisher, *The Life of Mahatma Gandhi,* p. 284.

use of public services; and he announced a three-day fast as a sign of atonement. This reaction alone sums up Gandhi's values, his style, and his manner of acting.

All of his life, the *Mahatma* used nonviolent action effectively. He organized his massive campaigns carefully. He insisted at the highest level of participants that they would conduct themselves with calm and dignity no matter the circumstances. He prepared the demonstrators by disclosing to them the risks they would be taking. He exhorted them, "to submit without protest to the penalty of disobedience (...) in obedience to the higher law of our being, the voice of conscience."[27] Notwithstanding all the precautions, the *Mahatma* knew the horror of the uncontrollable violence that was unleashed in the crowds that followed him.

Some say that this horror turned him more and more towards a restrained, indeed, individual action. In this perspective, it was said, he learned the effective use of long fasts. For example, in February 1917, there was a strike of the spinning mill workers who were demanding decent wages. When he saw their determination flagging, Gandhi undertook his first public fast to support them, and won. He then integrated this experience in his plan of battle.

Fifteen years later, he fasted again and forced the abandonment of a bill concerning voters' rights. This bill could have had the effect of dividing Indians according to religious denominations and of isolating the "outcasts" who were the untouchables. By September 1, 1947, just after the country had gained independence and was divided into two self-governing Dominions, Gandhi fasted again. This time it was to be a fast to death. He was protesting the outbreaks of violence in Calcutta, and he brought his own people back to reason within four days. Gandhi's fasts constituted a peaceful and very effective weapon; through them he caused the triumph of what he judged conformable to truth and love.

Though they started from a fervent desire for purification, Gandhi's fasts, like Esther Blondin's, aimed at reforming and

---

[27] Gerald Gold, *Gandhi a Pictorial Biography,* p. 67.

harmonizing human relations. One example is a fast that the *Mahatma* undertook, of which the purpose was "heart prayer for purification of myself and my associates for greater vigilance and watchfulness in connection with the *Haryian* cause;"[28] that is, the untouchables. Gandhi risked death in these singular combats, but that was his way of giving his life faithfully to his mission.

He made of the nonviolence he practiced, "the finest quality of the heart,"[29] and the instrument par excellence of reconciliation. "The soldier of nonviolence may give the supposed enemy a sense of right and bless him. His prayer for himself will always be that the spring of compassion in him may ever be flowing..."[30] Gandhi proscribed from nonviolence every vengeful intention and every thought of hatred. This was why he admitted that "unless there is hearty cooperation of the mind, a mere outward observance will be simply a mask, harmful both to the man himself and to others."[31]

Such love grows in a big heart. "I have the privilege of claiming many Englishmen as dearest friends,"[32] he said. He also had enemies among the British, but he maintained honest relations with them. The *Mahatma* knew how to distinguish between a person and his actions, even the most reprehensible. He excluded all divisions and all bitterness from his struggle. It was in risking this choice right to the end that he met his death. He murmured, in the hearing of the assassin who had just shot him, "*Hey Rama* (Oh, God)!"[33] Gandhi returned to his source. It was a source from which he had never ceased to draw the nonviolence which he identified with "the largest love."[34]

---

[28] *Ibid.*, p. 107.

[29] Mahatma Gandhi, *The Collected Works of Mahatma Gandhi, XLVI*, p. 2.

[30] Louis Fisher, *The Essential Gandhi. His Life, Work and Ideas,* p. 332.

[31] *Ibid.*, p. 318.

[32] Gerald Gold, *Gandhi a Pictorial Biography,* p. 82.

[33] Louis Fisher, *The Life of Mahatma Gandhi,* p. 4.

[34] Mahatma Gandhi, *The Selected Works of Mahatma Gandhi,* vol. 6, Shriman Narayan Editor, Ahmedabad, 1968, p. 154.

# HÉLDER CÂMARA

Like Mohandas Gandhi and Esther Blondin, Dom Hélder Câmara also lived his prophetic mission with a serenity formed of long practice of disarmament and nonviolence. "I've learned (...) that opposition helps us more than praise. It encourages humility (...) We must even welcome calumny, especially calumny we can't answer, as a way the Lord has of moving us ahead along the road of poverty." [35] The Bishop of Recife knew in Whom he had placed his faith and he followed the same road...

He experienced the lack of support of his Brazilian confrères. Despite the loneliness which resulted, he never spoke a word of blame or disparagement against those who sidelined him. Dom Hélder Câmara resolutely adopted this attitude and the conduct of his long life testifies to his sincerity.

The peaceful way in which he conducted his prophetic struggle was nevertheless built on justice. He said it was necessary to face the injustices because they "are a form of violence... the basic violence, violence number 1." [36] About this world, ravaged by exploitation and oppression, he had no illusions. But, as he said, "while I do not believe in armed violence, I am scarcely so naive as to think that brotherly counsel and pathetic appeals are enough to make socioeconomic structures tumble like the walls of Jericho." [37] So he stressed the active aspect of his fight. He borrowed a term from his friend of Taizé, Pastor Roger Schutz, "the violence of pacifists." [38] Dom Hélder Câmara was tireless in practising this violence of pacifists, and of encouraging others to do so. Everywhere he went, he called people to it. His stand on issues was very clear, "I don't like (...) the word 'pacifism'. It sounds too much like 'passivism'. And if it means peace at any price — even at the price of injustice or servitude, for oneself or others — then that of course will never do." [39]

---

[35] Hélder Câmara, *Questions for Living,* pp. 69 and 71.

[36] Id., *Spiral of Violence,* pp. 29-30.

[37] Id., *Revolution through Peace,* p. 37.

[38] Id., *The Conversions of a Bishop,* p. 179.

[39] Id., *Questions for Living,* p. 88.

According to him, there are no favourable conditions for exercising nonviolence which is a thousand leagues from submission or fear: "Don't forget (...) the aim of nonviolence is to force even a violent enemy to yield (...), but it also means that you don't wait until your adversary has been converted to nonviolence! This is why nonviolence is something for today, not for tomorrow!"[40] Esther Blondin too understood that very well. Certainly the risk was great and failure was possible, indeed was sometimes evident. But Dom Hélder Câmara's conviction was not weakened for all that. "If you think violence is an evil, you should also believe that only nonviolence can stop it (...) so give the energy you're not spending in the army to nonviolence and action as a means of resolving conflicts and furthering justice."[41] The cost is considerable as is love. However, it opens on a new world, because "sacrifices accepted in nonviolence are a better preparation for the future and for reconciliation than sacrifices imposed by violence."[42]

## OSCAR ROMERO

Oscar Romero opted for the same values. In April 1978, a popular organization sought refuge in his cathedral. The archbishop's first concern was to ensure the safety of those involved. He sent an emissary to the country's President. Then he rejoined the occupants who were under siege from the law enforcement troops. His message in a nutshell was that the love of Christ "excludes all resentment, all hatred."[43] He did not give in to violence in spite of untenable situations, and the increase of terrorism in his own diocese. To the guerrilla groups and to those who advocated violent solutions, he sent a call to understanding. "Nothing violent can be lasting. There are still human perspec-

---

[40] *Ibid.*, p. 96.
[41] *Ibid.*, p. 89.
[42] *Ibid.*, p. 94.
[43] James R. Brockman, *The Word Remains,* p. 104.

tives of reasonable solutions. And above all there is the Word of God, which has cried to us today: reconciliation!"[44]

If this reconciliation did not go hand in hand with a never-ending struggle for justice in truth, it would have been a counter-witness to the Gospel, according to this prophet. That is why he wrote in one of his pastoral letters, "The peace in which we believe is the product of justice. Violent conflicts (...) will not disappear until their last roots disappear."[45] Oscar Romero was not gentle towards the minorities who exploited the people. His constant and pitiless condemnation was, nevertheless, free of all bitterness.

His words sought to bring together those whom hatred divided: "the denouncements of the left against the right and the hatred of the right for the left appear irreconcilable, and those in the middle way say (...) be tough on them both (...) because there can be no love at all where people take sides to the point of hating others. We need to burst these dikes, we need to feel that there is a Father who loves us all."[46] He was the first to risk that reconciliation to which he called his people. He did it in a style analogous to that of many prophets. On October 11, 1977, he wrote to his countryman and confrère, Bishop Revelo: "I think it is a brotherly duty of candor to write you that your words in the synod of bishops, published here (...) have bewildered the priests and the people who are more conscious of our pastoral policy and only have cheered those who defame the Church (...) The rejection is general in your regard, although I have tried to lessen it by exhorting not to judge in advance and to wait for you to explain your meaning (...) I think that just now you suffer personally (...) You can be sure I will give you my complete backing. But out of faithfulness to our pastoral policy in the archdiocese, I would have to demand a satisfactory explanation of the matter."[47] This is typical of Oscar Romero's writing, and it bears witness to a nonviolence as active as it is effective.

---

[44] *Ibid.*, pp. 214-215.

[45] *Ibid.*, p. 130.

[46] *Ibid.*, p. 214.

[47] *Ibid.*, p. 84.

The archbishop's forgiveness reached out as much to his calumniators as to his assassins! Shortly before his death he confided to a journalist, "You may say, if they succeed in killing me, that I pardon and bless those who do it."[48] No more than Esther Blondin, did this prophet hold anything against those who were plotting his death. He was both disarmed and combative, nonviolent and uncompromising, adamant and conciliatory. He died just after giving the homily in which he had said, "May this body immolated and this blood sacrificed for men nourish us also, so that we may give our body and our blood to suffering and to pain, like Christ, not for self, but to give concepts of justice and peace to our people."[49]

## MARTIN LUTHER KING

From the very beginning of his prophetic mission, Martin Luther King spoke like Oscar Romero. "Blood may flow in the streets of Montgomery before we receive our freedom, but it must be our blood that flows and not that (...) of our white brothers,"[50] he said to his followers. When a first victory punctuated those interminable months of passive resistance, he prepared his people for possible reprisals. Workshops were held to help the blacks of the city: "He urged everyone to return to the buses on a nonsegregated basis the next day. Then Martin made a final appeal for restraint and courtesy (...) He said, 'We must seek an integration based on mutual respect. As we go to the buses, let us be loving enough to turn an enemy into a friend.'"[51]

In 1960, he organized liberty rides to obtain racial integration in the buses and terminals in the Southern United States. He warned the volunteer travellers, both black and white that

---

[48] *Ibid.,* p. 223.

[49] *Ibid.,* p. 220.

[50] Lerone Bennett, *What Manner of Man,* p. 98.

[51] Coretta Scott King, *My Life with Martin Luther King, Jr.,* pp. 146-147.

they "must develop the quiet courage of dying for a cause."[52] He was not far from reality. These volunteers bore the harassment and the blows of enraged segregationists wrecking the buses they were riding. Martin Luther King reacted in the only way he knew, nonviolently. He called this nonviolence a powerful and righteous weapon because "it does not seek to defeat or humiliate the opponent, but to win his friendship and understanding."[53]

He was creative in his choice of active nonviolence. In 1963, he was recruiting volunteers for his nonviolent army. He composed a formula for the ceremony of commitment. "Observe with both friend and foe the ordinary rules of courtesy (...) Refrain from the violence of fist, tongue or heart."[54] Like Esther Blondin and so many of the prophets, the black leader was not satisfied with outward disarmament or superficial pacifism. He appealed to the heart of his people. From the wellsprings of his heart and from his relationship to Christ, he drew on wonderful reserves of spontaneity. "With every ounce of our energy we must continue to rid this nation of the incubus of segregation. But we shall not in the process relinquish our privilege and our obligation to love."[55]

This privilege, which is also a risk, shadowed several events in his life. After the first attempted assassination, he said this of his aggressor, "This person needs help. She is not responsible for the violence she has done me. Don't do anything to her; don't prosecute her; get her healed."[56] This echo of the Gospel in our own day was not an isolated statement in the life of the Baptist Minister. One day, in public, some white ministers from Alabama discredited him and his movement. He told them he had only one desire. He expressed the hope "that circumstances will soon make it possible for me to meet each of you, not as

---

[52] Lerone Bennett, *What Manner of Man,* p. 126.

[53] Martin Luther King, Jr., *Stride toward Freedom,* p. 102.

[54] Lerone Bennett, *What Manner of Man,* p. 135.

[55] Martin Luther King, *Strength to Love,* p. 40.

[56] Coretta Scott King, *My Life with Martin Luther King, Jr.,* p. 170.

an integrationist or a civil rights leader, but as a fellow clergyman and a Christian brother."[57]

Martin Luther King tried to bring together and to rebuild broken bridges between people without, certainly, denying the rights of truth and justice. In his eyes, "forgiveness does not mean ignoring what has been done or putting a false label on an evil act. It means, rather, that the evil act no longer remains as a barrier to the relationship."[58] He was capable of such freedom only because he was able to recognize that, "the evil of the enemy — neighbour (...) never quite expresses all that he is."[59] This belief he shared with Esther Blondin. Martin Luther King walked his chosen way to the end convinced that only nonviolence inflamed by love could reconcile people. He said, "this is the only way to create the beloved community."[60]

Prophets engaged in real battles astonish us by their voluntary and unconditional disarmament. They attack without hate, fight without bitterness, and, to the end, they risk their hearts. Their fidelity has no limits; their way is without return because it leads to the future... to a better future.

[57] *Ibid.,* p. 228.
[58] Martin Luther King, *Strength to Love,* p. 35.
[59] *Ibid.,* p. 36.
[60] *Ibid.,* p. 40.

## Chapter 5

# A Prophetic Future

*I saw the birth of the little community of the Daughters of Saint Anne... little did I foresee one day its fortunate members doing good in a faraway land.*

Esther Blondin

*We shall never go too far.*

Dom Hélder Câmara

Sometimes we associate prophets with destiny as oracles or fore-tellers of the future. This way of understanding their discernment distorts the meaning of their mission. Their mission turns them towards a better world, here and now, for all people. The future inhabits the prophets like a living and vibrant hope which stirs them to action. It mobilizes their disciples and the crowds they gather. This is an essential aspect of their mission and it relates to the creativeness in their lives. The future forms the inspiration they bequeath to their contemporaries and to the generations that follow them.

## The Hope That Moves to Action

It was in this sense that Esther Blondin was a woman of the future. As a matter of fact, she gave evidence of the hope that was in her from the very beginning of her project. When Father Archambault and Bishop Bourget told her the risks and dangers of her venture, she said simply, "God wants to do it all."[1] Not that she was expecting an intervention from Him that would dispense her from acting, history shows the contrary. She proved, rather, to be a dynamic and creative leader. She was urged on by her thirst for justice and her fervent hope to gather round her like-minded young women. They shared her convictions, ready to commit their lives "for the glory of God and the salvation of souls." Together they educated children and the youth of Vaudreuil and proclaimed to them the Good News of the Gospel. Thus, they doubly opened up the future to them.

Through this concrete service, Esther and her companions

---

[1] *Positio*, pp. 328 and 455.

contributed significantly to 19th Century Québec society and the Church. They provided a way out of illiteracy and its consequent underdevelopment. The community spread quickly and soon expanded[2] to St. Genevieve to take charge of another school in October 1851.[3] The rapid growth of the young community led to a real housing shortage and a large scale moving in the summer of 1853. Esther's commitment was such that it created, nourished and fulfilled hope for a better future for her own people.

Soon, however, the foundress found herself in the heat of persecutions that swooped down on her and threatened the stability of her work. In those crucial years, she continued to rely on God with hope, as the following letter testifies: "It is not that I believe that God wills all that has been done and said, and all that is still being said and done; but He is nòt interfering, He allows it: that is sufficient for me; I expect from His infinite goodness the solution to this matter."[4] A few months later she foresaw her final dismissal from office. She expressed her deep inner conviction in a letter to her bishop: "There are such varying incidents at the present time that one has to keep one's eyes ever fixed on the Divine Polaris (...) I have to keep continually on my lips, and even more in my heart, these words (...) 'I placed my hope in you, Lord, and I shall not be eternally confounded.'"[5] The foundress, treated in the community as though she had disappeared, did not become discouraged. The strength of her hope even enabled her sisters to recover and to pursue their common mission.

---

[2] Father Paul Loup Archambault mentioned in one of his letters to Bishop Bourget, dated November 28, 1848, that 38 young women had asked to be admitted to the new community. See Sister Marie Jean de Pathmos, S.S.A., *Dossier sur la vie et les vertus,* p. 77.

[3] St. Genevieve is located about 30 kilometers from Vaudreuil on the Island of Montreal.

[4] *The Correspondence of Mother Marie Anne,* Letter to Sister Marie Jeanne de Chantal, February 1858, pp. 138-139.

[5] *Ibid.,* Letter to Bishop Bourget, July 5, 1858, pp. 158-159.

# The Shared Dream

It is to be noted that, at the same moment, the community entered a period of great expansion. It was able to start co-educational schools outside of Québec. In 1858, it established itself in Victoria, British Columbia, and soon spread up the Island and over to the Mainland. Eight years later, the foundress, still ardently seeking "the glory of God and the salvation of souls," was rejoiced at seeing her sisters leave for Oswego, an industrial city in New York State. Surely such missionary impetus could not have been extraneous to the secret desires of the foundress. In the United States, "in less than twenty years, the Sisters of Saint Anne had assumed the direction of seventeen parochial schools and one large boarding school."[6] Esther Blondin once confided to Sister Marie Emilienne that "those mixed classes were the realization of her fondest hopes."[7] She was 77 when the sisters went to Juneau, Alaska, and the annals of the community recorded her joy on that occasion.[8] It was said of these pioneer sisters that they had a great affection for the foundress and that they hung her photograph in their community room.[9] One of them wrote to her: "On September 8, the thirty-seventh anniversary of our foundation, I made an imaginary visit to our houses of Quebec, the United States, and British Columbia, and I thought: Our Mother Foundresses could have entertained the high hopes or even foreseen the possibility of making foundations in these countries; but, certainly, they never could have looked forward to a foundation in the territory of Alaska which was unknown to the world at the time. And yet, my very dear Mother, it is an accomplished fact, your daughters have a house here."[10]

[6] Sister Marie Jean de Pathmos, S.S.A, *A History of the Sisters of Saint Anne,* p. 308.

[7] *Ibid.,* p. 312.

[8] See Id., *Dossier sur la vie et les vertus,* pp. 709-710.

[9] See Id., *A History of the Sisters of Saint Anne,* p. 331.

[10] Letter from Sister Marie Théodore, *A History of the Sisters of Saint Anne,* September 12, 1887, p, 331.

Esther Blondin's prophetic intuitions were fulfilled by her daughters. [11] As the years went by, she was filled with the wonder of the harvest which grew so mysteriously: "I saw the birth of the little community of the Daughters of Saint Anne. I was a witness to its first years. For all the happiness which flooded my soul then, little did I foresee that one day I would see its fortunate members doing good in a faraway land." [12]

The knowledge of the fruitfulness of the community justified the hope of the foundress who still lived in obscurity. "For a tree to grow and bear fruit," she had said, "the roots must be hidden in the earth." [13] The last thirty-two years of her life were lived in silence. One of her daughters said: "Her role in the community was so hidden that I found out only several years after entering the novitiate that she was the foundress, and that, after God, my happiness of being a Sister of Saint Anne was thanks to her." [14] There is an abundance of such testimony... when distinguished persons sometimes visited the community of sisters at the motherhouse in Lachine. They would presume that the foundress was dead and all the while she was present in the assembly.

Yet Esther Blondin continued to trust her daughters. Her habitual kindness was well-known. She always said that everybody has a good side that makes up for any blame a person might deserve now and then. [15] In like manner she looks to the future through the eyes of the youngest among her sisters. Sister Marie Adrienne tells that as a novice she was not always mature in her behaviour. Embarrassed by her giddiness, she went to apologize to the foundress. Sister said, "She received me with motherly

---

[11] This community aspect of her mission does not minimize the fact that she was personally prevented from putting her prophetic gift into action. In this, she appears to be a prophet prematurely dejected. Jesus of Nazareth met this same tragic destiny.

[12] *The Correspondence of Mother Marie Anne,* Letter to Sister Marie de la Providence and her sisters, July 16, 1876, p. 205.

[13] *Positio,* pp. 588-589.

[14] *Ibid.,* p. 589.

[15] See *Ibid.,* p. 494.

118

kindness and did not speak a single word of reproof. 'What do you think of such youthfulness', I said on leaving. 'I think that our dear novices are the hope of the community."[16] Those were the heartfelt thoughts of her who was considered a useless burden, yet always entrusted her daughters to God. "Be very sure that I do not forget you in my humble prayers. It will be a very sweet duty to recommend you to God, you and your dear companions and your pupils, that he may bless you all."[17] The frequent letters of the aging foundress were always filled with hope.

## The Spirit of Easter

Her own personal journey from then on was a pascal one that defied all expectations and took on itself the bursting forth of all her designs. "Do not worry about a thing," she counselled one of her former pupils, "unite your sufferings to those of Christ."[18] That was how she herself had been for a long time, radiant with the peace of the Resurrection. Speaking of her own death, she said, "As for me, I think of it very often and it seems to me that it is not far off. My health is becoming more and more precarious. I shall never regain the energy I am losing; but I often say to God *'Fiat.'*"[19] She even entrusted to God the final word about her own life. "If you only knew how good God is," she said to one of the sisters during her last illness, "I have not the slightest fear about going to Him."[20] Lying, intrigue and disgrace caused her downfall and made a drama of her life, yet Esther grasped from a pascal perspective the meaning of all that passed on the stage of her life.

On January 2, 1890, she forgave Father Maréchal one last

---

[16] *Ibid.,* p. 592.

[17] *The Correspondence of Mother Marie Anne,* Letter to Sister Marie Martine, August 15, 1888, p. 222.

[18] *Ibid.,* Letter to Mrs. J.H. Roy, September 20, 1875, p. 200.

[19] *Ibid.,* Letter to Sister Marie de Bonsecours, August 9, 1888, p. 220.

[20] *Positio,* p. 599.

time and she accepted her death freely. With these two acts she made an offering in harmony with her mission. Her 441 daughters worked in 42 missions across North America, including British Columbia and Alaska, where they were the first women religious.[21] The foundress had handed on to them her prohetic spirit. They could now continue to spread and to open the future to thousands of young people and adults.

This fecundity, nevertheless, went hand in hand with a tragic destiny that survived her. Thus, one of the sisters said that after the death of the foundress, she received a notebook that had belonged to her. The general superior told her to hand it in and she never saw it again.[22] The general assistant was responsible for the disappearance of a notebook also. It was the one in which Father Aristide Brien wrote the personal interviews he had had with Esther Blondin between 1872 and 1875.[23] A few years later the general secretary confirmed that certain compromising documents had "disappeared from the archives of which she was in charge, and that she never saw them again."[24] Now only the major authorities had direct access to the archives. In January 1894, when Sister Marie de l'Assomption, one of the pioneer sisters, was nearing death, someone tried to make her say that Esther Blondin had not founded the community. This she firmly denied. These facts and others show how far the light of the foundress was deliberately put under the bushel basket. Such destructive action, however, was not to win over her prophetic gift.

---

[21] See *Positio,* p. 444, and Sister Mary Margaret Down, S.S.A., *A Century of Service,* p. 113.

[22] See *Positio,* p. 638.

[23] See Sister Marie Jean de Pathmos, S.S.A., *A History of the Sisters of Saint Anne,* pp. 215-216.

[24] *Positio,* p. 638.

# The Breakthrough of a Mission

Some prophets bask in glory even in their lifetime. Not so Esther Blondin. She was to remain in the shadows for thirty more years. Those decades that followed her death still assimilated her into the group called "Mother Foundresses," no more.[25] It is likely that this was because the sisters in authority had remained much the same. They were all from St. Jacques or around there, and consequently they were the spiritual daughters of Father Louis Adolphe Maréchal. Those who esteemed Esther Blondin, or who recognized her mission, usually kept their own counsel.

However, mention must be made here of Sister Marie Louise du Sacré Cœur, superior at the motherhouse from 1903 to 1909. She spoke out publicly about the foundress, and asked all those who knew her to put their testimony in writing. Sister Marie Irène succeeded, on her part, in collecting and compiling an impressive quantity of documents on Esther Blondin. To do this, she made good use of her influence as prefect of studies and as general secretary.[26] Some priests at that time also spoke of the foundress. In 1917, Father Urgel Demers, chaplain of the motherhouse, took the risk of offering the novices a series of conferences on her. The professed sisters who heard about them asked to hear the same conferences. Not far from there, at the convent on St. Joseph Street in Lachine, the chaplain, Father Henri Deslongchamps, had his own idea. He decided to interview Esther Blondin's contemporaries with whom he was in daily contact. On April 18, 1920, he presented to the community the fruits of his research and his reflections. The chroniclers reported on this, "The senior sisters disclosed with emotion that it was the first time they had heard our foundress praised, the first time they

---

[25] On the use of this expression, an official one, see Sister Marie Jean de Pathmos, S.S.A., *Dossier sur la vie et les vertus,* pp. 625-626. This was how Esther Blondin and her companions of the first profession were called.

[26] Sister Marie Irène was appointed to the office of the prefect of studies in 1892. She took charge of it four years later until she was elected general secretary in 1914.

had had the consolation of hearing someone who... made her loved and appreciated."[27]

In October 1919 there was the election of Mother Marie Léopoldine, the first general superior who was not from St. Jacques. Despite this, however, signs of a new era were not forthcoming for many more years. The first biography of Esther Blondin was published in 1935; but it could not give a full account of historical facts. The biographer had to avoid placing the former chaplain, Father Maréchal, in a bad light.[28] With the passage of years however, the whole emphasis began to change. The chapter of 1937 called for the first steps to be taken in Rome, with a view to the canonization of Esther Blondin.[29] This posthumous radiance, part of the paradox of her life, is at the very heart of Christian faith. It is often the lot of those who accompany Jesus of Nazareth and fight the good fight of his prophetic mission. They share in His glory, which is life overflowing. This mystery sometimes falls back into visible, historical reality. It is revealed particularly in the breakthrough of certain missions.

There is a sense of pascal paradox in the growth of the community after the death of Esther Blondin. Her daughters went to the Yukon in 1898. Before the end of the century, the novitiate, opened in Victoria in December 1889, had sent out thirteen young women newly professed.[30] Over the next decades the community established foundations in Japan, Haiti, Chile and Cameroon, pursuing its mission of Christian education. In doing

---

[27] *Dossier sur la vie et les vertus,* Chroniques du Vieux Couvent de Lachine, p. 623.

[28] On this subject, see Sister Marie Jean de Pathmos, S.S.A., *Dossier sur la vie et les vertus,* p. 628, note 35. Father Frédéric Langevin, S.J., is the author of the book entitled *Mère Marie-Anne, Fondatrice de l'Institut des Sœurs de Sainte-Anne, 1809-1890.*

[29] On the interval between the death of Esther Blondin and the first steps to introduce the cause of her canonization, Rome demanded a full investigation and concluded that there was no connection between the interval and any intrinsic facts about the life of the foundress. See Sister Marie Jean de Pathmos, S.S.A., *Dossier sur la vie et les vertus,* p. V.

[30] See Sister Marie Jean de Pathmos, S.S.A., *A History of the Sisters of Saint Anne,* p. 238.

this, the sisters sometimes risked becoming involved in new and pressing needs: the advancement of women in Africa, the conscientization and support of youth in the Third World in their struggle for justice. There were, also, the integration of immigrants into their adopted countries, the respect of the rights of students, the sick, and many others.

Could the heritage left by Esther Blondin to future generations, besides the witness of her life that the universal Church is now recognizing,[31] be the haunting need to serve humanity? Could her heritage also be the prophetic, non-conformist, even subversive character of her mission which is still able to inspire new risks? Would it not be her daughters who work now for a better, more human future, not limiting themselves to support services, necessary though these be? And, could her heritage also be all those men and women who find within themselves a kinship with her at the heart of their commitment for justice? Evidently, her mission goes on.

# The Future Opened by the Prophets

## MOHANDAS GANDHI

Mohandas Gandhi would no more envisage an end of his enterprise than would Esther Blondin. For himself he said, "All I can claim is that I am sailing in that direction without a moment's stop."[32] In 1909 he spoke of a hope, one that would mobilize all the energies of his being. Succinctly expressed, it says, "To believe that what has not occurred in history will not occur at all is to argue disbelief in the dignity of man."[33] It was from

---

[31] It is from the historical dossier written for the cause of canonization of Esther Blondin that the majority of facts and documents were taken for this book. This dossier meets all the new procedures for the causes of Saints as promulgated by Pope John Paul II in 1983. It is the work of the community historian, Sister Marie Jean de Pathmos (Laura Jean), S.S.A.

[32] Louis Fisher, *The Life of Mahatma Gandhi,* p. 493.

[33] *Ibid.,* p. 126.

this perspective that the *Mahatma* took up the cause of "the friendship of the whole of humanity,"[34] the Hindu-Moslem brotherhood, and the "voluntary interdependence"[35] of India and Great Britain. He had a dream he was struggling to achieve: "I shall work for an India in which the poorest shall feel it is their country in whose making they have an effective voice, an India in which there will be no high class or low class of people, an India in which all communities shall live in perfect harmony (...) neither exploiting, nor being exploited."[36] So he was aspiring to something much higher than treaties or constitutions. He wanted, for his country: "a cultural regeneration and spiritual renaissance which would give it inner freedom and hence, inevitably, outer freedom; for if the people acquired individual and collective dignity they would insist on their rights, and then nobody could hold them in bondage."[37]

Like Esther Blondin and all other prophets, Mohandas Gandhi became inseparably one with his mission, and it was to cost him his life. After the bombing attempt in 1934, he said, "Let those who grudge me what yet remains of my earthly existence know that it is the easiest thing to do away with my body. I have no strong desire for martyrdom, but if it comes it will help my work for the *Haryians*;"[38] that is, the untouchables. The prophet's life found meaning only in the mission that polarized it. At 77, he decided to travel through all the devastated regions of his country, defying all the common-sense laws of self-defence. These devastated regions resulted from the massive killings in Calcutta, the Hindu massacres at Noakhali, and the vengeance taken on the Moslems of Bihar, the riots in the Punjab, and the revolution that raged in a northwestern province. "I am prepared for any eventuality. 'Do or die' has to be put to the test here. 'do' here means that Hindus and Moslems should learn to live

---

[34] Robert Payne, *The Life and Death of Mahatma Gandhi,* p. 487.
[35] Louis Fisher, *The Life of Mahatma Gandhi,* p. 285.
[36] Robert Payne, *The Life and Death of Mahatma Gandhi,* p. 605.
[37] Louis Fisher, *The Life of Mahatma Gandhi,* p. 132.
[38] Robert Payne, *The Life and Death of Mahatma Gandhi,* p. 457.

together in peace and amity. Otherwise, I should die in the attempts."[39] Faced with the Hindu-Moslem problem that resisted him and would always resist him, he said, "I am helpless (...) That is why I said that it has passed into the hands of God."[40] This certitude, which Esther Blondin also had, was no stranger to freedom, nor to the serenity which marked the closing years of his life. He said of the last fast he undertook in response to his interior voice, "It was only when in terms of human effort I had exhausted all resources... that I put my head on God's lap... God sent me the fast."[41] Gandhi was firmly convinced that God accompanied him to the place of sacrifice. There, he offered himself for a unified, free India, ready to fulfill its spiritual mission in the contemporary world. He felt that his death was near, and during the last days of his life he questioned himself. He wondered what he must undertake in such a climate of violence which was tearing his country. He confided to a friend "it is all in the lap of God."[42] When death came, the name of God came to his lips, as though to give God the last word.

"There was so much more for him to do. We could never think that he was unnecessary or that he had done his task,"[43] said Nehru at Gandhi's death. In fact, he who had been "a motherly father for multitudes"[44] indeed had not finished his work. After his death, thousands upon thousands of his disciples all around the world pursued his mission. They treasured his heritage of nonviolence, of freedom, of dignity, and of commitment to a more friendly world. "Future historians will probably regard him as one of those rare men who come at the end of historical epochs and by their very presence announce the beginning of a new dispensation."[45]

---

[39] Louis Fisher, *The Life of Mahatma Gandhi,* p. 449.

[40] *Ibid.,* p. 246.

[41] *Ibid.,* p. 494.

[42] Robert Payne, *The Life and Death of Mahatma Gandhi,* p. 586.

[43] *Ibid.,* p. 595.

[44] Louis Fisher, *The Life of Mahatma Gandhi,* p. 338.

[45] Robert Payne, *The Life and Death of Mahatma Gandhi,* p. 606.

# HÉLDER CÂMARA

That is how Dom Hélder Câmara appears, too. The Council was an outstanding experience for him, that literally swept him into a mission of worldwide dimension. It rekindled his hope in the very plan of God: "God has taught the Church of Vatican II to trust man. Instead of… losing patience with him when, with incredible daring, he rushes off in all directions, the Church exults and proclaims that by acting in this way, man is only following the Divine Command to rule nature and complete the work of creation."[46] The bishop discovered new and unheard of perspectives of his struggle, in the manner of Esther Blondin and many of the prophets. He said, "Human betterment — the struggle against the causes of injustice, the conquest of dignity — is the right reason for human beings to cooperate in achieving the salvation and redemption for which the Lord gave His life."[47] Here was a vision far removed from short-term dreams or causes intertwined with petty self-seeking.

The hope that sustained the Brazilian bishop constantly revitalized his commitment. "There are still many things going badly, (…) so this is scarcely the moment to stop getting involved or, therefore, to stop hoping!"[48] It helped him face obstacles and count on God. "I hope not only for the help of God, who surely will not abandon His masterpiece of creative evolution to its fate; I find a source of hope, too, in man's intelligence and common sense."[49] Relying on his faith in God and in people, Dom Hélder Câmara repudiated paralyzing fear that blocked horizons. He went ahead: "It isn't the progress of science, technology, and the economy that we should be afraid of when it comes to the future of faith, but the progress of selfishness and injustice (…) faith has a future because there is, and always will be, a future

---

[46] Hélder Câmara, *Revolution through Peace,* p. 25.
[47] Id., *Questions for Living,* pp. 34-35.
[48] *Ibid.,* p. 65.
[49] Id., *Revolution through Peace,* p. 90.

126

for more justice and a greater communion of brothers and sisters."[50]

He walked this road without offending the religious or political beliefs of those with whom he made common cause. Believers or atheists, capitalists or communists, Christians or Agnostics, leftwing or rightwing, he recognized the prophetic Spirit in them: "When I look around myself, it's so clear that a great number of people who call themselves believers have no hope for peace, for justice and for happiness of all here on this earth; and that many who do not know God or believe in God are involved in battles to the point of risking their lives... the Spirit of God breathes everywhere."[51] The bishop who ignored barriers that separate people, was particularly close to the rising generations. "God gives me the job of loving the young and of believing in them."[52] In the face of tomorrow's challenges, he trusted them. "They are on the road to the future (...) We should like them to reproduce our own experiences. But have no fear, they will receive from us the best of what we have been. Be more attentive to what they proclaim."[53] Esther Blondin would certainly have echoed those sentiments.

The future that Dom Hélder Câmara faced was not the secret of a diviner. Rather, the bishop spoke of it as the outcome of his daring commitment. He challenged the future wherever he went: "If all of us, while mindful of eternal life, demand human conditions for human beings on earth; if all of us make up our minds to go beyond mere aid and carry out human and social advancement, then it will soon become clear that the hour of change has struck."[54] He thought this change was possible because of the solidarity of minority groups. In his eyes they were "a force more powerful than nuclear power itself."[55] This was

---

[50] Id., *Questions for Living,* pp. 23 and 25.

[51] *Ibid.,* pp. 18 and 20.

[52] Id., *Race against Time,* p. 77.

[53] Id., *Questions for Living,* p. 21.

[54] Id., *Revolution through Peace,* p. 138.

[55] Id., *The Conversions of a Bishop,* p. 213.

127

not the language of a man with a great future, but of a prophet who was roused by the Spirit. Despite the sufferings and pain he encountered within the Church, he prepared a brighter future by encouraging Christians to keep up the fight: "I'm an old bishop, (...) and I have enough confidence to ask you never to resign yourself to the weaknesses, the compromises, perhaps even the treachery of the Church nor ever to despair of the Spirit of the Lord who never ceases to dwell in the Church." [56] The future was always open to Dom Hélder Câmara even when he said he was beginning "to prepare to reach the final destination" or when he foresaw a violent death "for the sake of peace in the world and harmony between peoples." [57] Even today, the retired bishop travels throughout the world and gathers "Abraham's minority groups". They are the men and women on every continent who are working for a better world and one of greater justice.


## OSCAR ROMERO

In the same vein, his confrère Bishop Oscar Romero, wished to "make of El Salvador a land of brothers and sisters, all children of one Father," [58] a land that would become "the antechamber of the Kingdom beyond." [59] Like many prophets, he tried to realize that dream in the present. He, the shepherd who tirelessly drew his people together communicated his hope to those who could act. In 1979, on his return from the Latin-American Episcopal Conference in Puebla, he addressed a gathering. They were politicians, capitalists, professional and Christian specialists. "You have the key to the solution. But the Church gives you what you cannot have by yourselves: the hope, the optimism to

---

[56] Id., *Questions for Living,* p. 32.
[57] Id., *The Conversions of a Bishop,* p. 215.
[58] James R. Brockman, *The Word Remains,* p. 215.
[59] *Ibid.,* p. 185.

struggle, the joy of knowing that there is a solution, that God is our Father Who keeps on impelling us."[60]

The point was to go ahead and to keep on going even though the road was rough and dangerous. In San Salvador, at that time, the government faced a crisis, the military high command opposed the junta, ministers and senior officials resigned, chaos gained ground. Yet, the bishop's message remained the same. On January 6, 1980, he repeated it: "At this moment, I want to restate my conviction, as a man of hope (...) We all have the duty to seek together new channels and to hope actively, as Christians (...) what must be saved before all is our people's march toward liberation."[61]

The archbishop invited his countrymen to make some radical and daring structural reforms. The success of his cause, contrary to all appearances, seemed to be guaranteed. His assurance sounds like an echo from Esther Blondin a century before. "Whoever believes in Christ, even under the oppressor's boot, knows that he or she is a victor and that the definitive victory will be that of truth and justice."[62]

In the fight, Oscar Romero always had at heart a wider perspective than immediate results. It made his commitment more daring and more relevant: "Christ's redemption liberates a crippled world. People are not fulfilled until they are able to free from sin those who are sinners, and from death those who are dead (...) Blessed are those who work for the political liberation of the world, keeping in mind the redemption wrought by him who saves from sin and saves from death."[63] Before such an open and liberated future, he became very serene. Later, the discovery was made of some explosives in his cathedral. He said that from then on, instead of fear he had greater confidence. For

---

[60] *Ibid.*, p. 150.

[61] *Ibid.*, p. 195.

[62] Oscar Romero, *A Martyr's Message of Hope. Six Homilies by Archbishop Oscar Romero*, p. 137.

[63] *Ibid.*, p. 92.

the one who trusted God, God would protect from any evil.[64] Any ultimate evil, that is.

Like many prophets, the archbishop would pay with his life for fidelity to his mission. But his hope would remain unshaken and joined forever to the future of his people. Two weeks before his death he granted a telephone interview to a correspondent from the Mexican newspaper the *Excelsior*. He told him: "I have often been threatened with death. Nevertheless, as a Christian, I do not believe in death without resurrection (...) from this moment I offer my blood to God for the redemption and for the resurrection of El Salvador (...) if God accepts the sacrifice of my life, let my blood be a seed of freedom and the sign that hope will soon be reality."[65] In his life, as in his death, Oscar Romero pursued his mission to the end. And since that day, Monday, March 24, 1980, despite the assassin's bullet, he still lives. He continues to inspire, to sustain his people of El Salvador whom he called together so often and loved so much. He still kindles the ardor of committed Christians and especially the youth, those whom he called "the rich hope of the Church in Latin America."[66]


## MARTIN LUTHER KING


Martin Luther King's struggle, just as concrete as Oscar Romero's or Esther Blondin's, assured a breakthrough to the future for his own people. His widow Coretta affirmed that he believed that "God had decided to use Montgomery as the proving ground for the struggle and the triumph of freedom and justice in America."[67] He also believed, that "we who dedicate ourselves to God are His instruments in that glorious

---

[64] See Id., *Assassiné avec les pauvres*, p. 176.

[65] James R. Brockman, *The Word Remains*, p. 223.

[66] Oscar Romero, *A Martyr's Message of Hope. Six Homilies by Archbishop Oscar Romero*, p. 78.

[67] Coretta Scott King, *My Life with Martin Luther King, Jr.*, p. 119.

130

struggle."[68] The prophet was aware that God was with him. And so was Coretta. All his major decisions, in crises or in very difficult times, followed consultation with her, and hours of prayer. Prayer enlightened his perspective, affirmed his hope and impelled him to action. "God (...) would defeat His own purpose if He permitted us to obtain through prayer what may come through work and intelligence."[69] Nevertheless, he leaned on God in the times of his greatest defeats. "Faith in the dawn arises from the faith that God is good and just. When one believes this, he knows that the contradictions of life are neither final nor ultimate."[70] This hope, which makes him resemble Esther Blondin, strengthened his commitment, as it does those who follow him fervently. "I have the personal faith that mankind will somehow rise to the occasion and give new directions to an age drifting rapidly to its doom (...) In a dark confused world the Kingdom of God may yet reign in the hearts of men."[71] Such conviction sustained both his fight and his option for nonviolence.

The prophet had a long and far-reaching vision. He received the Nobel Peace Prize in Oslo in December 1964. And in his speech he shared his wonderful convictions: "I accept this award today with an abiding faith in America and an audacious faith in mankind. I refuse to accept the idea that man is mere flotsam and jetsam in the river of life which surrounds him. I refuse to accept the view that mankind is so tragically bound to the starless midnight of racism and war that the bright daylight of peace and brotherhood can never become a reality."[72] For him, as for every prophet, believing in people was neither an error nor a stupidity, unless God Himself was mistaken. Through his mission, which guided him always further along this path, Martin Luther King became a national symbol of freedom. He discovered that

---

[68] *Ibid.*, p. 92.

[69] Martin Luther King, *Strength to Love,* p. 122.

[70] *Ibid.*, p. 49.

[71] Thilo Koch, *Fighters for a New World,* p. 202.

[72] Coretta Scott King, *My Life with Martin Luther King, Jr.,* p. 13.

"justice is indivisible."[73] Gradually, his vision expanded to international solidarity, to which he wants to bring his own and his people's contribution. "The American Negro of 1967 (...) may be the vanguard in a prolonged struggle that may change the shape of the world."[74]

With an eye to the future, he assured his flock of the vitality of the younger generations. Barely 30 himself, he brought into the directorship of his movement, several university students. Then he went into the ghettos of the Northern United States. Here his dream was to win over the young radicals who already made common cause against injustice.

But Martin Luther King's personal future was to follow the pascal route. His widow Coretta stated that "Martin had set Good Friday, April 12, 1963, for the day that he and some other leaders would provoke arrest by breaking the injunction. He had deliberately chosen that day because of its symbolic and religious significance."[75] It was of his own free will, like Esther Blondin, that he changed his sufferings into a creative force. In the Baptist church in Birmingham, a bomb killed four little girls — an act of vengeance on his movement. His reply was, "unearned suffering is redemptive."[76] It was this conviction, the profound side of his self, that prepared him for the ultimate outcome of his mission. In 1962, six years before his death, he foresaw his violent end. In the church in Albany, Georgia, he said, "... it may get me crucified. I may die. But I want it said even if I die in the struggle that 'He died to make men free'."[77] Coretta said that he felt that the complete gift of himself would be a source of inspiration to others. He would in this live part of the resurrection in which he believed.[78]

Martin Luther King did not think of his mission as coming

---

[73] Martin Luther King, *The Trumpet of Conscience,* p. 24.

[74] *Ibid.,* p. 17.

[75] Coretta Scott King, *My Life with Martin Luther King, Jr.,* p. 222.

[76] Martin Luther King, *Strength to Love,* p. 141.

[77] John Ansbro, *Martin Luther King, Jr.: The Making of a Mind,* p. 97.

[78] See Coretta Scott King, *My Life with Martin Luther King, Jr.,* p. 320.

to an end. When death caught him, he was preparing a demonstration in support of the Memphis garbage collectors and sewer workers. The demonstration occurred as planned, in spite of his assassination. Over the years, Martin had gathered a throng of disciples with whom he shared his mission. To this day, they all walk hand in hand towards a future where "one day men will rise up and come to see that they are made to live together as brothers."[79]

The prophets were men and women looking towards the future. They each opened up history in a precise direction, that of abundant life for all human beings. They communicated to their followers an active hope, that neither failure nor death could weaken. All of them had a far-reaching vision. They worked to build loving relationships, justice, and peace or salvation for the whole world. Their horizons extended into the "true promised land"[80] that Esther Blondin spoke about. This was a land they dreamed about, made credible, and started to make real all at the same time.

---

[79] Martin Luther King, *The Trumpet of Conscience,* p. 77.

[80] *The Correspondence of Mother Marie Anne,* Letter to Sister Marie Joachim, July 2, 1876, p. 204.

# Conclusion

*Our Christian faith requires that we submerge ourselves in the world.*

Oscar Romero

The dynamism of prophets leads them to act and to speak unanimously and disparately. These men and women do not belong to any particular category of persons. They are rooted in history and shaped by a given culture. They share the lives of their contemporaries: the questions, yearnings, limitations and even the failures.

Then, in what are they unique? It is in their sensitivity to the needs of the most deprived and oppressed in their midst. It is the commitment and the resourcefulness they bring to making their world a more just place to live. It is in their manner of speaking in the bitter confrontations where they are led, always honest, sensible and decisive. Prophets are people with a passion for unity, and they bring an active nonviolence to the very situation where the human fabric has been torn and where they meet their tragic destiny. This aspect of prophetic dynamism is radically different from the dynamism of revolution, which is an essential element of class struggle. Finally, the living hope which indwells the prophets makes them leaders for now and tomorrow in the march towards a better life.

Prophets live in a close, personal relationship with God, Who seems to beg for their action and from Whom they draw the strength to practise nonviolence to the point of forgiveness. They put their trust in God as partners in a dream of abundant life for all. Is this the God of men and women of good will? He certainly was the God of Jesus of Nazareth and of His disciples.

In this perspective, to speak of the prophetic dynamism of Esther Blondin is to recognize her commitment to the service of justice: she responded to the need for alphabetization, education and christian growth of the children and youth of her milieu at a time when they needed it most. That is, at a time when the degree of poverty, ignorance and christian anemia of Quebec's rural French-Canadian population had become unbearable.

To speak of the prophetic dynamism of Esther Blondin is to recall the language she spoke: did she not dare to override the sexist prejudice of her time the better to serve the rights of the young? Did she not stand to defend their rights and those of her sisters when they were threatened? Did she not prefer straight talk to self-interested calculations?

To speak of the prophetic dynamism of Esther Blondin is to identify her destiny with that of all prophets. For if she had neither acted nor spoken as she did, she would not have been subjected to the tragic destiny which was hers.

To speak of her prophetic dynamism is also to discover, under appearances which time would now label old-fashioned, the choice she made in favor of active non-violence and unity.

To speak of her prophetic dynamism is, finally, to recognize the future she opened for her people and the universality emanating from her message.

Though she does belong to the prophetic line, Esther Blondin is nevertheless distinct from such great prophets as Martin Luther King, Gandhi, Romero or Câmara, because her particular mission was as foundress. We can even affirm that it is through this mission that she lived her prophetic dynamism and transmitted it to her daughters who have spread it across time and space. In this sense, she really has a communal originality which is essential and which marvelously underlines the collective dimension inherent in all prophecy.[1]

Yet some people ask what Esther Blondin's prophetic dynamism would look like today. This question, fortunately, has no answer. But it reminds us that we do not have to repeat what she did in her day. The same can be said of all the prophets, who showed proof of undergoing personal growth in the course of their lives. In this regard, Louis Fisher affirms that Gandhi became "reconciled to more state participation in economic

---

[1] See Pierre Gilbert, "Vrai et faux prophète" in *Lumière et vie,* 165, Novembre-Décembre, 1983, pp. 21-31.

affairs."[2] We also know that Câmara became aware of the root causes of underdevelopment during Vatican II.

Prophets are not models to be imitated, but they certainly are great sources of inspiration for what is at stake in the world today. "Life is so short,"[3] said Esther Blondin. How right she was! In many places the rights of people are still denied or severely restricted. Exploitation or colonialism is still practised by individuals or groups in society as well as in the Church. Yes, we still have need of prophets, true prophets, not those who predict a catastrophic end, but rather, those who tell us that now is the time for action, even dangerous action. Now is the time to speak out, even the unacceptable message. After all, does the Gospel say anything less?

---

[2] Louis Fisher, *The Life of Mahatma Gandhi,* p. 327.

[3] *The Correspondence of Mother Marie Anne,* Letter to Bishop Bourget, July 5, 1858, p. 159.

# Biographical References

# ESTHER BLONDIN

1809  April 18    Birth of Marie Esther Sureau dit Blondin at Terrebonne, Quebec.

1830             Esther went to the village convent in Terrebonne as a boarder. While working in the service of the Sisters of the Congregation of Notre Dame, she learned to read and write.

1831             She entered as a postulant in the Congregation of Notre Dame and became a novice with the name of Sister Saint Christine.

1833             Because of her failing health, she was sent home to her family in the spring.

1833  May        Esther arrived in Vaudreuil to lend a helping hand to Suzanne Pineault, a teacher in the parochial school. The latter had once been in the novitiate of the Sisters of the Congregation of Notre Dame.

1838             After the departure of Suzanne Pineault, Esther took on the responsibility for the Vaudreuil school which she transformed into an academy. According to the legislation of the time, this fact made her responsible for training teachers for the small surrounding schools.

| | | |
|---|---|---|
| 1843 | | The pious association of the Daughters of Mary Immaculate was founded in Vaudreuil's St. Michel's parish. Esther became its president, a position she kept until 1848. |
| 1847 | | She fell ill in the summer and went through a period of soul-searching. |
| 1848 | | During Lent, she revealed to the pastor of Vaudreuil, Father Paul Loup Archambault, her plan to found a religious community of educators who would see to the needs of poor country children in mixed schools. |
| 1848 | June | At the request of the pastor of Vaudreuil, Esther presented her project to Bishop Ignace Bourget, bishop of the diocese of Montreal. He said to her, "Try..." |
| 1848 | September | Esther and the six companions she had recruited made a retreat in preparation for the official opening of the novitiate. Esther was made responsible for the group and would carry various responsibilities from then until 1850. |
| 1849 | August 15 | First investiture in the new community. Esther was given the name Sister Marie Anne. |
| 1850 | September 8 | With the pronouncing of the vows of Esther and four of her companions, the community was officially established under the name of Daughters of Saint Anne. Esther became its first superior. |
| 1851 | October 10 | At the request of the pastor, Father Louis Marie Lefaivre, the Daughters of Saint Anne opened their second convent-school at St. Genevieve. |
| 1852 | June 21 | Bishop François Norbert Blanchet, bishop of Oregon City, visited the young community and appealed to it for missionaries. |

| 1853 | August 22 | The community and novitiate became established in St. Jacques de l'Achigan where Father Louis Adolphe Delphis Maréchal became their chaplain; later, (1858) he would be named pastor of the parish and ecclesiastical superior of the congregation. |
|---|---|---|
| 1854 | August 19 | Esther Blondin resigned, on the order of Bishop Ignace Bourget. Falling ill, she spent a few weeks in the infirmary. |
| 1854 | November 2 | She went to St. Genevieve, where she stayed until July 1858 as directress of the convent-school. |
| 1855 | | On June 20, she made a private vow to honour the Immaculate Conception, and on the following August 5, a special promise to Saint Anne for the benefit of all her daughters. |
| 1855 | September | Esther made a long spiritual retreat, the Exercises of Saint Ignatius, and she began a perpetual fast, which she ended on October 28, 1858, on the order of her superior. |
| 1857 | | She offered to go to the mission which was about to open on Vancouver Island. |
| 1858 | April 7 | The first contingent of sisters left for Victoria in Western Canada. |
| 1858 | July | Following a decision of Bishop Bourget, the authority of the community withdrew Esther Blondin from St. Genevieve. This gesture proved to be the final destitution of the foundress. During that summer, she was also isolated in St. Ambroise de Kildare. |
| 1858 | September | Esther Blondin was recalled to the motherhouse in St. Jacques and her name does not even appear on the list of general community appointments. Esther called that year of 1858-1859, her zero year. |

| 1859 | | Esther Blondin was given two assignments: sacristan in the parish church, where Father Louis Adolphe Delphis Maréchal was pastor, and clothier for the sisters at the convent. |

| 1861 | | She was sacristan and doorkeeper at St. Jacques. |

| 1863 | March 14 | The community received from Rome a "Decree of praise" in which St. Jacques was designated as the place of foundation in 1850. |

| 1864 | October 17 | The foundress was named to Lachine which became the headquarters of the community... She would be successively portress, linen-keeper, sacristan, infirmarian, and in charge of ironing. Father Napoléon Maréchal, brother of Louis Adolphe Delphis, was chaplain of the convent. |

| 1866 | September | Esther Blondin was named superior-directress at St. Genevieve. The authorities sent her there with the intention of obtaining from Father Lefaivre the direction of the hospice he was planning to open in his parish. As the project proved to be premature, Esther was recalled from St. Genevieve even before the end of the school year. |

| 1866 | | The daughters of Esther became established in Oswego, New York, in the United States. In less than twenty years, they would have opened 17 schools in that country. |

| 1869 | April-May | The foundress spent a short time in St. Genevieve. Her superiors sent her there with the same intention they had had in 1866. Since the Pastor Lefaivre judged it inopportune to pursue his project immediately, Esther was recalled to Lachine. |

| 1872 | | The chapter of the community elected Esther Blondin as general assistant. Two months later, an act of the general council recognized her as a councillor only. This last function was, in fact, purely nominal. |
|------|---|---|
| 1873 | August 15 | On the 24th anniversary of the first investiture in the community, an address was read to "the foundresses." |
| 1878 | | At a new chapter, Esther was elected general councillor. She was totally ignored. |
| 1884 | May 2 | Pope Leo XIII officially approved the community under the name of Sisters of Saint Anne. The Roman document also sanctioned the error of the 1863 decree which had named St. Jacques de l'Achigan as the place of foundation. That error was corrected thirteen years after the death of the foundress. |
| 1886 | September | The foundress rejoiced over the establishment of her sisters in Juneau, Alaska. |
| 1890 | January 2 | Esther Blondin dies in the infirmary of the motherhouse in Lachine at the age of 80 years. |

(From a chronology drawn up by Sister Louise Roy, S.S.A., in *The Correspondence of Mother Marie Anne,* pp. 10-11.)

# HÉLDER CÂMARA

1909   February 7   Birth of Hélder Câmara at Fortaleza in the Brazilian *Nordeste.*

1922   Birth of the Brazilian Communist Party; it became outlawed in 1935.

1923   Hélder entered the minor seminary with the intention of becoming a priest.

1930   Some Brazilian lieutenants, in an effort to shake the oligarchy of their country, started a revolution and brought into power Getulio Vargas, whom they declared President.

1931   August 15   Hélder Câmara was ordained priest at age 22. The period of his life that was just beginning would be dominated by educational tasks and marked by the ideology of integralism, which was a Brazilian form of fascism, of hitlerism, and of the corporationism of Salazar. Hélder worked in the *Nordeste.*

1936   January   Hélder left the *Nordeste* and went to Rio de Janeiro where the archbishop, Cardinal Sebastao Leme, asked him to give up militant integralism; this he promptly did. At the request of the cardinal, Hélder Câmara became director of the Department of Education for the State. He would become successively a specialist in the Ministry of Education, member of the Superior Council for Education and responsible for religious education in the archdiocese. It was in Rio that Dom Hélder came face to face with the misery of the *favelas* and that he discovered the dimensions and the very deep causes of the problems of education.

1946

Dom Hélder began to get involved with Catholic Action, at the request of Cardinal Jaime de Barros Câmara (no relaion to Hélder) who had succeeded Cardinal Leme.

1947

He obtained from his archbishop the authorization to resign from both the Ministry and the Superior Council of Education, to devote his time to what he considered more priestly works. That year he created the national secretariat for Brazilian Catholic Action. He was named general chaplain of that movement.

1948    February

Dom Hélder was deeply impressed by the assassination of Gandhi.

1950

General secretary of the holy year in Brazil, he organized and accompanied a pilgrimage to Rome with 1,300 Brazilians. The unbelievably bad conditions made this an epic voyage.

1952

He became auxiliary bishop of Rio de Janeiro.

1952-1964

From the creation of the Conference of Brazilian Bishops, Hélder Câmara was its general secretary. Pioneer of collegiality, Hélder worked to establish this conference with Bishop Giovanni Battista Montini, in Rome.

1955

He organized the International Eucharistic Congress of Rio de Janeiro with dazzling splendour. It was during this event that he met Cardinal Pierre Gerlier of Lyon, France. The latter asked him a question, "... why do you not put this organizational talent that the Lord has given you to the service of the poor?'' That question proved to be the turning point in Hélder Câmara's life. After the congress, he occupied himself with searching for a solution to the housing problems of the *favelas*. Despite a partial failure, he succeeded in attracting the attention of the civil authorities to that situation.

1962    October 11    He took part in Vatican II in Rome, the council which would close after ten public sessions, on December 8, 1965. Hélder Câmara discovered there the international roots of underdevelopment.

1964    March 13    He was named archbishop of Olinda and of Recife, following the death of Cardinal Jaime de Barros Câmara.

1964    April 1    A military coup d'état overthrew the Brazilian government. This revolution became institutionalized... the struggle against "subversion" began and touched particularly those who denounced injustice. There were numerous cases of disappearances, of torture, of assassinations and restrictions of freedom.

1966    The beginning of the travels of Hélder Câmara: he responded to the invitations he received. From that time, he travelled the world about five weeks of every year in order to awaken the international conscience to the drama of the Third World.

1968    He participated in the Conference of Latin-American Bishops at Medellin in Columbia. This conference, summoned and opened by Paul VI himself, marked the beginning of the "theology of liberation."

| | | |
|---|---|---|
| 1968 | October | Hélder Câmara created in Recife a movement of active nonviolence, "Action, Justice and Peace". This movement which aimed at creating moral pressure for freedom within Brazil would have no future, but the archbishop would realize on the international plan what was impossible for him on the national level. |
| 1970 | May | At the Palace of Sports in Paris, Hélder Câmara denounced the tortures perpetrated in his own country. From that moment, a campaign of defamation was unleashed against him in Brazil and he was condemned to "civil death" when he was silenced. Hélder Câmara did not receive much support from the Brazilian episcopate. |
| 1973 | | He received the Popular Peace Prize from Oslo, Norway. This prize was, in fact, a protestation against the Nobel Prize which that year had been granted to Henry Kissinger (U.S.A.) and Le Duc Tho (North Vietnamese). |
| 1985 | | At the age of 76, the Archbishop of Olinda and Recife went into retirement and announced his intention to pursue his mission while touring the world to promote justice. |

(From Hélder Câmara, *The Conversions of a Bishop. An Interview with José de Broucker*.)

# MOHANDAS GANDHI

1869    October 2     Birth of Mohandas Karamchand Gandhi, at Orbandar, India.

1885    November     He was wedded to Kastruba Makanji. They would have four sons during their lifetime.

1888    September 4     At Bombay, Gandhi embarked for England where he would pursue studies in Law.

1891    June 10     Gandhi was admitted to the bar and he returned to India on the 12th of the same month.

1892    April     Gandhi, having difficulty in building a clientele, left for South Africa as a judicial councillor for Dada Abdulla and Co.

1893    June     While on his way to Pretoria, he received the order to disembark from the train and he vowed to devote himself to active nonviolent resistance.

1901    October     Gandhi left South Africa and returned to India.

1902    December 25     As he had not yet succeeded in building an adequate clientele, he returned to South Africa with his family.

| 1908 | January | First prison term following a strike to protest a law that obliged Indians to a special registration in South Africa. Gandhi entered upon his mission. |
|------|---------|------|
| 1914 | July 18 | Gandhi left South Africa, never to return. |
| 1916 | February 6 | Gandhi spoke out at the University of Benares. |
| 1917 | April 10 | Gandhi went to Patna to find out for himself about the problems of the indigo workers in Champaran. The problems would be settled in August. |
| 1919 | | He founded a periodical, *The Young India,* of which he was editor-in-chief. |
| 1919 | April 13 | Massacre of Amritsar. Gandhi announced his penitential three-day fast. |
| 1924 | September 17 | He undertook a fast of twenty-one days for the unity of Hindus and Moslems. |
| 1930 | March 12 | Gandhi started the Salt March from Sabarmati to Dandi. |
| 1930 | April 6 | He broke the Salt Law on the shores of Dandi. A month later, he was imprisoned, without trial, at Yeravda. |
| 1932 | September 20 | Gandhi protested, by a fast until death, against the establishment of a separate college for untouchables. |
| 1933 | November 7 | He undertook a tour of India that would last ten months. |
| 1935 | June 25 | A Hindu threw a bomb onto Gandhi's car at Poona. |

| 1939 | July 23 | Gandhi wrote a letter to Hitler, but the letter was never delivered. The same thing happened on December 24, 1941. |
| 1942 | August 8 | Congress voted the motion "Get Out Of India." Gandhi launched a national campaign under the slogan "To Win or To Die." |
| 1946 | | That year was marked by violence in India. In November, Gandhi undertook a four-month tour through eastern Bengal that was being ravaged by civil war. |
| 1947 | August 15 | Gandhi was in Calcutta. British India became independent and would henceforth be divided into two Dominions: India and Pakistan. Riots and violence broke out among the various Indian communities. |
| 1948 | January 20 | A bomb exploded at Birla House where Gandhi was living. He was not wounded. |
| 1948 | January 30 | Gandhi was assassinated by a Hindu fanatic, Nathuram Godse. He was 78 years old. |

(From Robert Payne,
*The Life and Death of Mahatma Gandhi.*)

# MARTIN LUTHER KING

| | | |
|---|---|---|
| 1929 | January 15 | Birth in Atlanta, Georgia, of Martin Luther King, Jr. |
| 1944 | | Martin entered Morehouse College, University of Atlanta, to prepare for a career in Law. While pursuing his studies, he opted for the pastoral ministry, like his father. |
| 1947 | | Martin was named assistant pastor in his father's parish. He began to mingle with the masses of black people, and in order to have greater sharing in the workers' lives, he chose to work for two summers at the Railway Express Company and at the Southern Spring Bed Mattress Company. |
| 1948 | June | He finished his studies at Morehouse College, and that fall, he went to the Crozer Faculty of Theology in Chester, Pennsylvania. |
| 1950 | | Martin Luther King came into contact with the thought and the writings of Gandhi. He was profoundly impressed by them. |
| 1951 | | He pursued further studies in philosophy at the University of Boston. It was in that city that he met singer Coretta Scott, his future wife. |

| | | |
|---|---|---|
| 1953 | June 18 | Martin married Coretta. They would have four children, two boys and two girls. |
| 1954 | August | The King couple settled in Atlanta. Martin became pastor of the Dexter Avenue Baptist church, and became involved in social action. |
| 1955 | June | He received his doctorate in philosophy with a specialty in theology. |
| 1955 | December 1 | On a bus in Montgomery, Rose Parks refused to give up her seat to a white person and was arrested by the police. Pastor King was asked to do something for the woman. It was decided to boycott the city buses for twenty-four hours. It was protracted to 382 days. Martin took the lead in this movement, from the start. |
| 1956 | January 30 | A bomb was thrown onto the gallery of the Kings' home. During that year, Martin began his tours in the Northern United States. |
| 1956 | December 21 | Racial segregation was abolished on buses, following a decision of the Supreme Court, and the boycotting of buses in Montgomery came to an end. |
| 1957 | May 17 | Martin Luther King organized the "Pilgrimage of Prayer" for black civil rights. It took place at the Lincoln Memorial. |
| 1957 | June 13 | Martin attempted to get the Federal government to become involved in the struggle of the blacks. He had a talk with Vice-President Richard Nixon. |
| 1957 | September 3 | On the occasion of his third arrest, he decided to remain in prison rather than pay a fine, in order to arouse public opinion for the black cause. |

| | | |
|---|---|---|
| 1957 | September 20 | A woman attempted to assassinate him in a store in Harlem. |
| 1958 | February | He went to India, on the invitation of Prime Minister Jawaharlal Nehru, friend of Gandhi. |
| 1960 | February 17 | He was arrested on suspicion of income tax fraud. A jury acquitted him on the following May 28. |
| 1961 | May 4 | The first "Voyage for Freedom" left Washington. Martin was part of the formation team that trained the nonviolent travellers. |
| 1963 | April 3 | He opened the campaign in Birmingham, Alabama, to put an end to segregation in stores, to establish proper working conditions, and to create a bi-racial committee. Police brutality, riots and demonstrations marked this campaign. |
| 1963 | April 12 | On Good Friday, King chose to make a peaceful demonstration, thus inviting arrest. |
| 1963 | August 28 | During the March on Washington, which had assembled 250,000 people, Martin uttered his famous speech, "I Have a Dream." |
| 1963 | November 22 | President John F. Kennedy was assassinated. Lyndon Baines Johnson succeeded him and almost immediately summoned Martin Luther King to discuss the racial problem. |
| 1964 | July | Riots broke out in Harlem and spread across the country. Martin was very concerned about it. |
| 1964 | December 10 | He received the Nobel Peace Prize in Oslo, Norway. |

| 1965 | August 6 | Following the campaign in Selma, Alabama, a bill was signed into law, giving blacks the right to vote. |
| 1966 | January | Martin and his family settled in one of the slums of Chicago. |
| 1967 | January | He publicly opposed the war in Vietnam and undertook the "Poor People's Campaign" to fight against the socio-economic causes of the black revolt. |
| 1968 | April 4 | Martin Luther King was assassinated in Memphis, Tennessee, where he was preparing a demonstration in support of the garbage collectors and sewermen of the city. He was 39 years old. |

(From Lerone Bennett, *What Manner of Man,* and Coretta Scott King, *My Life with Martin Luther King, Jr.*)

# OSCAR ROMERO

| | | |
|---|---|---|
| 1917 | August 15 | Birth of Oscar Arnulfo Romero y Galda in Ciudad Barrios, Salvador. |
| 1929 | | Oscar left school and became an apprentice carpenter. |
| 1931 | | He left his village for the minor seminary in San Miguel; he wanted to become a priest. |
| 1937 | | He entered the national seminary of San Salvador, and after seven months, his bishop sent him to study in Rome. |
| 1942 | April 4 | Oscar was ordained a priest in Rome where he stayed to pursue further studies. |
| 1943 | | He returned to Salvador and he undertook different ministries for several years: secretary of the diocese, school chaplain, editor of a diocesan weekly, pastor of a parish. |
| 1967 | | He was named to San Salvador, the capital of the country, and became secretary of the Conference of Bishops. |
| 1970 | June 21 | He was consecrated bishop and became auxiliary bishop of San Salvador. |

| | | |
|---|---|---|
| 1974 | October 15 | Oscar Romero was made bishop of Santiago de Maria. His eyes were opened to the plight of the peasants. He spent some time researching. |
| 1977 | February 22 | He became archbishop of San Salvador with the proven reputation of conservative and moderate. |
| 1977 | February 26 | General Carlos Humberto Romero (no relative) was proclaimed head of the Salvadorean government and succeeded to President Arturo Molina. |
| 1977 | March 12 | Father Rutilio Grande, S.J., personal friend of Oscar and deeply involved with the 30,000 peasants of his region, assassinated. |
| 1977 | March 13 | At the eight o'clock Mass, Oscar read a declaration of the bishops on human rights, and his homily was broadcast by radio on station YSAX. |
| 1977 | March 30 | He was much comforted by a private audience with Pope Paul VI in Rome. |
| 1977 | August 10 | He met with the President of the country and suggested measures to improve the Salvadorean situation. He demanded explanations, inquiries, and investigations into missing, exiled, or imprisoned persons. |
| 1977 | October | At the synod of bishops, in Rome, Bishop Revelo discredited the Salvadorean pastoral ministry. He would be named Bishop Romero's auxiliary at the beginning of 1978. |
| 1978 | February 14 | Oscar Romero, having become increasingly well-known at the international level, received an honorary doctorate at the University of Georgetown in Washington, D.C. |

| 1978 | September 4 | Because of his solidarity with the people, he refused to participate in the reception given by the Nuncio for the inauguration of Pope John Paul I. |
| 1978 | November | Bishop Romero was nominated for the Nobel Peace Prize. He did not receive it. |
| 1979 | January 27 | Until February 13, he participated in the Conference of Latin-American Bishops in Puebla, Mexico. |
| 1979 | May 7 | He had a private audience in Rome with Pope John Paul II who encouraged him to be bold, courageous and prudent. |
| 1979 | October 15 | Coup d'état in Salvador. The President fled to Guatemala and a military junta succeeded him. |
| 1980 | January | Violence in Salvador increased significantly. The prophet's struggle intensified. |
| 1980 | February 17 | Oscar Romero wrote to the American President, Jimmy Carter, to demand the cessation of his military aid to the Salvadorean government and the restoration of legitimate auto-determination to his country. |
| 1980 | February 18 | A bomb destroyed the diocesan radio station which broadcast Bishop Romero's weekly homilies. |
| 1980 | March | Oscar Romero was interviewed by telephone from Guatemala, by the reporter from the Mexican newspaper, *Excelsior*. He spoke of his impending death. |
| 1980 | March 24 | He was assassinated at the end of his homily, while saying the 6 p.m. Mass. He was 62 years old. |

(From James R. Brockman,
*The Word Remains: A Life of Oscar Romero*.)

# BIBLIOGRAPHY

## 1. Esther Blondin

*The Correspondence of Mother Marie Anne,* compiled and annotated by Louise Roy, S.S.A., translated from the French by Eileen Gallagher, S.S.A., Lachine: Saint Anne Edition, 1977.

Down, Margaret, S.S.A., *A Century of Service: A History of the Sisters of Saint Anne and their Contribution to Education in British Columbia, the Yukon and Alaska,* Victoria, B.C.: The Sisters of Saint Anne, 1966.

*The First Rules of the Sisters of Saint Anne,* presented by Louise Roy, S.S.A., translated from the French by Florence Chevalier, S.S.A., and Margaret Flanagan, S.S.A., Lachine: Saint Anne Edition, 1979.

Marie Jean de Pathmos, S.S.A., *Canonisation de la servante de Dieu Marie-Esther Sureau dit Blondin (en religion Mère Marie-Anne), fondatrice de la Congrégation des Sœurs de Sainte-Anne (1809-1890), Dossier sur la vie et les vertus,* Rome: 1985.

Marie Jean de Pathmos, S.S.A., *A History of the Sisters of Saint Anne,* translated from the French by Sister Marie Anne Eva, S.S.A., New York: Vantage Press, 1961.

Nadeau, Eugène, O.M.I., *The Life of Mother Mary Ann Foundress of the Sisters of Saint Anne (1809-1890),* translated from the French by Sister Mary Camilla, S.S.A., Lachine: Saint Anne Edition, 1965.

*Positio super introductione Causæ,* Rome, 1975.

Pouliot, Léon, S.J., *Monseigneur Bourget et son temps,* tome III, L'évêque de Montréal, Montréal: Bellarmin, 1972.

## 2. Hélder Câmara

Broucker, José de, *Dom Hélder Câmara. The Violence of a Peacemaker,* New York: Maryknoll, Orbis Books, 1970.

Câmara, Dom Hélder, *The Church and Colonialism. The Betrayal of the Third World,* Denville, New Jersey: Dimension Books, Sheed and Ward Ltd., 1969.

Câmara, Dom Hélder, *The Conversions of a Bishop. An Interview with José de Broucker,* London: Collins, 1979.

Câmara, Dom Hélder, *Mille raisons pour vivre,* Paris: Seuil, 1980.

Câmara, Dom Hélder, *Questions for Living,* New York: Maryknoll, Orbis Books, 1987.

Câmara, Dom Hélder, *Race against Time,* London: Sheed and Ward Ltd., 1971.

Câmara, Dom Hélder, *Revolution through Peace,* New York: Harper and Row, Harper Colophon Books, 1972.

Câmara, Dom Hélder, *Spiral of Violence,* London: Sheed and Ward Ltd., 1975.

## 3. Mohandas Gandhi

Fisher, Louis, *The Essential Gandhi. His Life, Work and Ideas,* New York: Vintage Books, 1962.

Fisher, Louis, *The Life of Mahatma Gandhi,* New York: Harper and Brothers Publishers, 1950.

163

Gandhi, Mahatma, *The Collected Works of Mahatma Gandhi,* Delhi: The Publications Division, Ministry of Information and Broadcasting Government of India, 1967.

Gold, Gerald and Attenborough, Richard, *Gandhi a Pictorial Biography,* New York: Newmarket Press, 1983.

Payne, Robert, *The Life and Death of Mahatma Gandhi,* New York: E.P. Dutton and Co., 1969.

## 4. Martin Luther King

Ansbro, John, *Martin Luther King, Jr.: The Making of a Mind,* New York: Maryknoll, Orbis Books, 1982.

Bennett, Lerone, *What Manner of Man,* Chicago: Johnson Publishing Co., Book Division, 1964.

Dhombre, Pierre et Marie-Hélène Sigaut, *Prier avec Martin Luther King,* Montréal: Fides, 1980.

King, Coretta Scott, *My Life with Martin Luther King, Jr.,* New York: Holt, Rinehart and Winston Inc., 1969.

King, Martin Luther, Jr., *Strength to Love,* New York: Harper and Row Publishers, 1963.

King, Martin Luther, Jr., *Stride toward Freedom: The Montgomery Story,* New York: Harper and Row Publishers, 1958.

King, Martin Luther, Jr., *The Trumpet of Conscience,* New York: Harper and Row Publishers, 1968.

Koch, Thilo, *Fighters for a New World,* New York: G.P. Putnam's Sons, 1969.

# 5. Oscar Arnulfo Romero

Antoine, Charles, "Monseigneur Romero, victime de la peur des bien-pensants" in *Croissance des jeunes nations,* 217, mai 1980.

Brockman, James R., *The Word Remains: A Life of Oscar Romero,* New York: Maryknoll, Orbis Books, 1982.

Erdozain, Placido, *Archbishop Romero Martyr of Salvador,* New York: Maryknoll, Orbis Books, 1981.

Romero, Oscar, Archevêque de San Salvador, *Assassiné avec les pauvres,* Paris: Cerf, "L'Évangile au vingtième siècle", 1981.

Romero, Oscar, *A Martyr's Message of Hope. Six Homilies by Archbishop Oscar Romero,* Kansas City, Missouri: Celebration Books, 1981.

Romero, Oscar, *Voice of the Voiceless. The Four Pastoral Letters and Other Statements,* New York: Maryknoll, Orbis Books, 1985.

# 6. General Works

Development and Peace, *A Time to Speak Out,* Ottawa: July 1984.

Duquoc, Christian, *Jésus homme libre,* Paris: Cerf, 1973.

Gilbert, Pierre, "Vrai et faux prophètes" in *Lumière et vie,* 165, novembre-décembre 1983.

Goldberger, Pierre, "La réconciliation par la justice" in *Le Bulletin de l'Entraide missionnaire,* 3, septembre 1983.

Hétu, Jean-Luc, "Prisonniers d'opinion hier et aujourd'hui," in *Orient,* 185, janvier-février 1984.

Lemieux, Lucien, *Vie de l'Église (THL 3110),* cours d'histoire donné à la faculté de Théologie de l'Université de Montréal, septembre-décembre 1978.

Léon-Dufour, Xavier, *Dictionnaire du Nouveau Testament,* Paris: Seuil, 2ᵉ édition, "Livre de vie", 131, 1975.

Mattarollo, Rodolfo, "Qu'est-ce qu'un disparu?" in *Croissance des jeunes nations,* 233, novembre 1981.

Toulat, Pierre, "Disparition forcée et morale internationale" in *Croissance des jeunes nations,* 233, novembre 1981.

Imprimerie des Éditions Paulines
250, boul. Saint-François Nord
Sherbrooke, QC, J1E 2B9

*Imprimé au Canada — Printed in Canada*